A FIELD GUIDE TO
U.S. CONGREGATIONS

SECOND EDITION

Also by Cynthia Woolever and Deborah Bruce
From Westminster John Knox Press

Beyond the Ordinary: Ten Strengths of U.S. Congregations
Places of Promise: Finding Strength in Your Congregation's Location

A FIELD GUIDE TO U.S. CONGREGATIONS

Who's Going Where and Why

SECOND EDITION

Cynthia Woolever and Deborah Bruce

WESTMINSTER
JOHN KNOX PRESS
LOUISVILLE · KENTUCKY

U.S. CONGREGATIONS

© 2010 Cynthia Woolever and Deborah Bruce

The U.S. Congregational Life Survey was conducted in compliance with the American Association for Public Opinion Research's (AAPOR) Code of Professional Ethics and Practices, which may be found on the AAPOR Web site at www.aapor.org/ethics.

Book design by PerfecType, Nashville, Tennessee
Cartoons: © Chris Morgan, www.cxmedia.com
Cover design by Mark Abrams

Second edition
Published by Westminster John Knox Press
Louisville, Kentucky

This book is printed on acid-free paper that meets the American National Standards Institute Z39.48 standard. ∞

PRINTED IN THE UNITED STATES OF AMERICA

10 11 12 13 14 15 16 17 18 19 — 10 9 8 7 6 5 4 3 2 1

Library of Congress Cataloging-in-Publication Data

Woolever, Cynthia.
    A field guide to U.S. congregations : who's going where and why / Cynthia Woolever, Deborah Bruce. — 2nd ed., [new & expanded ed.].
        p. cm.
      ISBN 978-0-664-23514-7 (alk. paper)
    1. Parishes—United States—Case studies. 2. Pastoral theology—United States—Case studies. I. Bruce, Deborah. II. Title. III. Title: Field guide to United States congregations.
      BV700.W66 2010
      277.3'083—dc22

                                                                    2009033738

CONTENTS

ACKNOWLEDGMENTS

WE GIVE SPECIAL THANKS . . .

To Joelle Anderson, Hilary Harris, and Ida Smith-Williams, who helped us do the heavy lifting required by this big project.

To everyone else in Research Services, Presbyterian Church (U.S.A.) who contributed in countless ways to make this project happen: Jack Marcum (coordinator), Perry Chang, Susan King, Becki Moody, Jonathan Moody, Gail Quets, and Christy Riggs.

To research colleagues who directed the denominational oversamples for Wave 2: James Bowers, Laura Chambers, Roger Dudley, Rich Houseal, Destiny Shellhammer, and Marty Smith.

To colleagues who served as consultants: Jim Cavendish, Mark Chaves, Ann Deibert, Robert Dixon, Kevin Dougherty, Carl Dudley, Mary Gautier, Conrad Hackett, Kirk Hadaway, Trey Hammond, Dale Jones, Matt Loveland, Penny Marler, Herb Miller, Sharon Miller, Marcia Myers, Clay Polson, David Roozen, Scott Thumma, and David Voas.

To colleagues who helped lead the way during Wave 1: Jackson Carroll, Becky McMillan Haney, and Keith Wulff.

To international colleagues with whom we collaborated on the International Congregational Life Survey and whose earlier work set the stage for this project: John Bellamy, Keith Castle, Howard Dillon, Robert Dixon, Dean Drayton, Peter Kaldor, Ruth Powell, Tina Rendell, and Sam Sterling (Australia); Norman Brookes (New Zealand); and Phillip Escott, Alison Gelder, and Roger Whitehead (United Kingdom).

To the excellent staff of Presbyterian Publishing Corporation who support us in publishing our findings, particularly David Dobson, David Maxwell, and Vince Patton.

To our funding organizations and their officers: Chris Coble and John Wimmer, of Lilly Endowment Inc., and James Lewis, of the Louisville Institute.

And, most important, to the worshipers and their congregations who generously gave their time to help us update our one-of-a-kind picture of U.S. congregations.

CHAPTER 1

WHY A FIELD GUIDE?

We received two highly unusual field guides as gifts: One guide contained everything you could possibly want to know about cows; the other book recounted in detail everything about sport-utility vehicles, or SUVs. The guides were amusing and interesting. But these gifts raised a question for us: Why do we know *less* about U.S. congregations than we do about cows and SUVs? Aren't congregations, as one of the most enduring expressions of American religious life, just as important to comprehend as our automobiles and livestock? A search of bookstore shelves under "Field Guides" yielded more examples of research describing birds, plants, and animals. As researchers committed to understanding religion, we decided a field guide to congregations would add a valuable volume to the shelf.

America has always been known for its voluntary associations of all types. Research documenting how voluntary groups make use of resources, especially volunteers, abounds. Recent attention has focused on how voluntary groups respond to larger cultural changes as well as to changes in their more specific contexts. The most common and enduring of all voluntary organizations is the local church or congregation. When compared to other associations, congregations exhibit incredible strength and vitality. No other voluntary organization enjoys the degree of commitment and centrality in the life of its "volunteers" as does the local church or congregation. In fact, the depth of many members' and worshipers' commitment makes leaders and others sometimes forget that they indeed are volunteers. And these volunteers can and do vote with their feet!

What is unique about the congregation as a voluntary association? Congregations are like clay creatures—inventions of our own making, part of the social fabric, fulfilling quite ordinary human needs. Congregations are like common clay in another way because they possess the uncommon qualities of both extreme resiliency and fragility. We've heard stories about congregations and parishes that rose from the ashes—they were down to their last five members or their building was destroyed by fire, and they found a way to be reborn, stronger in mission than ever before. Others tell stories of David-like congregations slaying the Goliaths of poverty, despair, or injustice in their communities. We also recognize the stories of strong congregations, perhaps with thousands of members, destroyed by problematic personalities, theological splits, or other unnatural disasters—all signs of the paradoxical fragility and resiliency of congregational life.

Yet these vessels of clay are quite exceptional. They embody the sacred in an increasingly secular world. They demonstrate God's creative work in the world. Just as humans are clay creatures, filled with God's own breath, so congregations carry the breath of the divine in a hurting world. If we want to help congregations and parishes, don't we need to better understand this uncommon nature? If we are committed to the task of strengthening congregations and their leaders, aren't we partners with God in an uncommon calling?

Can We See More from the Pews?

Many people say they know what American worshipers find meaningful in a congregation. Reputable experts compile lists of qualities they believe contribute to "congregational vitality." Books advise congregations and parishes about priorities they should emphasize. Yet until recently, little evidence existed to paint an accurate picture of worshipers, congregations, and the American religious landscape.

Most worshipers believe their congregation is unique. In many ways they are right. Every congregation is a collection of one-of-a-kind individuals who make up a distinct group portrait. Each congregation's location is also unique: on a particular street, in a particular neighborhood, in a one-of-a-kind city or town or rural community. Certainly, the singular setting of a congregation shapes it in ways we do not fully understand. However, congregational leaders often use this uniqueness as an excuse for ignoring lessons that they can learn from others. Thus, changes that might increase their congregation's effectiveness never are considered.

While each congregation is distinctive, much about congregations is universal. Congregations share similar dreams and struggles. Committed to understanding congregational life, the authors worked with research teams from Australia, New Zealand, and England to study congregations and parishes in 2001. This international effort included 1.2 million worshipers in 12,000 congregations. Then, in 2008 and 2009, the authors conducted a second national study of congregations in the United States. American congregations that participated in the 2001 effort were invited again to survey their worshipers in the fall of 2008 or the spring of 2009. At the same time, a new nationally representative sample of congregations was invited to join the follow-up effort as well.

The study results you hold in your hands help us answer fundamental questions: *Who attends religious services? Why do they go? What makes American congregations and parishes work? What is the role of our culture and society in shaping the nature of congregations?* This volume describes "what is" and "who we are" in American congregations with updated data from the second wave of the U.S. Congregational Life Survey.

Why now? Many participants, stakeholders, and congregation watchers have a sense that we are in an "in-between" time—not too far from the past when most denominations and congregations were growing and the number of priests, pastors, and ministers

MYTH TRAPS

Myths are tempting assumptions about congregational life. If we believe the Myth Trap presented in each chapter, we will use the same old methods to achieve the same old results. Myths immobilize and trap us in dead ends, blocking us from fully living out the answer to our most important question: What is God calling us to be and do as a congregation?

met the demand. But we are certainly not fully in the future where present challenges have grounded new creativity in ministry. In this transition time, shifting from past to future, a general sense of unease prevails. Many leaders believe that some congregations are in denial about present-day realities. Other parishes and congregations that have moved beyond denial now face despair. Should leaders move forward to discernment, decision making, and action? Can we use our discomfort as motivation to open the door to new possibilities? We believe so.

Leading congregations has never been more challenging. The tasks and obstacles have never been more complex. Organizational problems, changes in the community, and rising expectations often undermine efforts by the most talented and charismatic of leaders. People demand better results from every institution they encounter, including their congregation and parish. Congregational leaders need the kind of reality-based analysis that leaders in growing, healthy, excellence-oriented organizations find helpful. This volume offers a similar reality-based view for religious leaders and worshipers.

The U.S. Congregational Life Survey

The scope of the U.S. Congregational Life Survey project is immense. Funded by generous grants from Lilly Endowment Inc. and the Louisville Institute, two national studies provide the largest and most representative profile of worshipers and their congregations ever developed in the United States. More than 500,000 worshipers filled out a survey during religious services.

Our efforts provide a comprehensive picture of America's worshipers (chapter 2) and the congregations or parishes where they worship (chapter 3). Further, the survey project explored four dimensions of congregational life—spirituality and faith development; activities and relationships within the congregation; community involvement; and worshipers' vision for the congregation's future. Chapter 4 examines the ways congregations and parishes help people grow in their faith through their worship life and other congregational activities. A second important area of congregational life—what happens inside the congregation—is reported in chapter 5. That chapter reports worshipers' participation in congregational groups, their sense of belonging, and their leadership roles. Community involvement is investigated in chapter 6, including services that congregations provide to the community and efforts to invite people to worship services and other congregational activities. Chapter 7 details some specific types of worshipers, such as frequent attendees and first-time attendees. The study findings in chapter 8 profile pastors—how they can be described demographically and how they lead congregations. Chapter 9 captures worshipers' views about the future directions of their congregation. Finally, chapter 10 reviews the key changes among worshipers and their congregations since 2001.

FAST FACTS

Knowing is not the same thing as doing. Unless crucial research facts lead to the question "If this is true, then what should our congregation do?" the new information may be interesting but irrelevant. In each chapter, the Fast Fact box provides signposts for congregations moving toward data-driven decisions. In view of the presented research facts, the reader should ask, "What steps could our congregation take to be more effective?"

Why conduct a new study? Continuous change occurs at the national and local levels. However, the key questions are "how *much* change?" and "what *kinds* of change?" Several factors generally drive change, including population shifts, technological innovation, financial fluctuations, new policies, and organizations and people adapting to new demands. Replicating the study allows us to assess the impact of societal changes since 2001 on congregational life.

One-time events are another source of change. These include out-of-the-ordinary circumstances such as the September 11 attacks on the World Trade Center, the Pentagon, and Flight 93. Worship attendance soared briefly after the September attacks.[1]

1. Results from a Gallup poll indicate that the percentage of Americans who reported attending church in the previous seven days rose to 47% immediately after the September attacks (up from 41%). But by the first anniversary (September 2002), the percentage had dropped to 43%, and by February 2003 it was down to 38%. See Jeffrey M. Jones, "Sept. 11 Effects, Though Largely Faded, Persist," at http://www.gallup.com/poll/9208/Sept-Effects-Though-Largely-Faded-Persist.aspx?version=print.

Because our first study occurred in April 2001, our original picture of American congregations was taken *before* this historic national tragedy. Our new data enable us to address this question: Are there any lasting effects on congregations or their worshipers?

The second U.S. Congregational Life Survey gave us the opportunity to look at change at the national level—for example, in the demographic profile of worshipers, the size of congregations, and the resources congregations have at their disposal. We wondered about general trends in worship styles, outreach efforts, and technology use. We also were able to investigate trends at a congregational level because some of the 2001 congregations participated again in 2008. For example, aspects that worshipers value most about their congregation may shift over time. If so, these shifting priorities may call for changes in staff portfolios, volunteer time, and finances.

How Is This Picture Different from What You've Seen Before?

The chapters that follow provide a view of the American religious landscape that is different from traditional views in a number of ways:

- *A large representative national sample of congregations and parishes participated in the study.* Previous studies of congregational life have been based on small samples or in-depth case studies. Because congregations involved in these previous studies may not be typical, results are not representative of all congregations. The U.S. Congregational Life Survey polled worshipers from every state across the country; from rural, suburban, and urban areas; from growing communities and communities in decline.

- *We asked the opinions of both leaders and worshipers.* Most previous studies have relied on the views and opinions of clergy or a single lay leader in participating congregations and parishes. The U.S. Congregational Life Survey records the voices of 500,000 people who regularly invest in congregational life through their participation in worship. Together with information from clergy, their views are the definitive source of information about congregations and parishes.

- *A broad range of denominations and faith groups took part.* Advice offered by consultants and other experts on congregational life is based on years of experience working with congregations. However, their observations are often limited to the range of congregations and parishes encountered in their work. This scientific research supplements these perspectives by offering a current snapshot of congregations based on a random sample of U.S. congregations. It provides an opportunity for all of us to test our own theories and the experiential advice being offered by consultants and denominational leaders.

- *Congregational health is envisioned as more than numerical growth.* Rather than relying on one measure of vitality, we investigated four fundamental areas of congregational life—spirituality and faith development; involvement in groups and leadership roles; community involvement; and future directions. Thus, congregations and parishes can see where their strengths are and where change may be needed in the multidimensional arena of vitality.

- *The experiences of worshipers in congregations of all sizes are included.* Too often researchers and congregational consultants select large congregations or megachurches, rapidly growing congregations, congregations with one-of-a-kind ministries, congregations in conflict, or congregations and parishes that are unique in some other way. This causes difficulties for leaders and attendees who attempt to apply the lessons in small or midsize congregations, in declining or stable communities, or in other settings. Our findings complement and qualify the congregational examples found elsewhere.

Many researchers see the search for common threads in congregational life across the diversity of U.S. faith communities as an impossible mission. Yet we believe there are common questions that all congregations and parishes face: Who are we? What is our mission? What do we believe? Do we welcome others? How do we do so? How do we relate to the community? How do we adapt to change while maintaining our core values? While the search for general trends is a difficult one, it is an essential requirement for congregations seeking greater health and vitality.

The Case for Data-Driven Decisions

Many factors can and should drive a congregation's decisions. Among those factors, leaders in various denominations and faith traditions use four with great frequency:

- *Theology-driven decisions.* For example, a congregation or parish believes in a God whose nature calls them to minister with refugees or people with HIV/AIDS or to embrace other caring actions.

- *Bible-driven decisions.* For example, a congregation believes in the Great Commandment and the Great Commission, which encourages compassionate efforts to help people in the community and invites others to a life-changing and personal relationship with Jesus Christ.

- *Spirit-driven decisions.* For example, a congregation believes in seeking and deriving direction from prayer or discernment that comes from a sense of being led by God's Spirit.

- *Tradition-driven decisions.* For example, a congregation believes in a high level of support to worldwide missionary efforts or intensive efforts to end racism in the community. These actions stem from the congregation's heritage or how the congregation has done things in the past.

A fifth factor can influence a congregation's decisions—information or data. Unfortunately, many congregations make fewer data-driven decisions than their current reality requires, depending instead on other factors, such as the four described above. What happens if a congregation or parish leaves out of its decision-making equation information about the changed nature of the community in which they are located? What happens if a congregation ignores the data that reveal a change in its congregational leadership and identity? These congregations move faithfully forward making decisions based on nonexistent realities. Moving forward on used-to-be truths or half-truths produces disappointing and sometimes disastrous outcomes.

Congregations operate out of mental maps based on a complex mix of these and other factors. These mental maps direct congregations as much as road maps direct the traveler. The destination points and plotted highways leaders have constructed for congregational life send them on charted journeys that too often are resource consuming and unsatisfying. What if parish and congregational leaders revised their mental maps? What if they made new maps based on an accurate picture of the current landscape?

Who Speaks for Congregations?

Reality matters, and what people do with facts matters even more. The Tacoma Narrows Bridge built over Puget Sound, Washington, collapsed only four months after it was constructed. What happened? At the time, the reason for the collapse was a mystery. When engineers and architects studied the bridge and determined "nothing was wrong," they decided to rebuild the bridge in exactly the same way. Theodore von Kármán, a distinguished Hungarian-born physics professor, heard of the decision and warned the builders that if they rebuilt the bridge in the same way, the span would fall again. His recommendation was based on an understanding of moderate winds—a harmonic principle known today as "von Kármán's vortex." Initially his warning was met with suspicion and skepticism. Looking for ulterior motives, they asked him: "What is your interest in this? Who do you represent? For whom do you speak?"

In his rich Hungarian accent, von Kármán replied: "I speak for the wind."[2]

Who speaks for congregations? Facts matter! Basing actions on an accurate assessment of reality is critical. This book invites leaders and worshipers to gain a fresh perspective on which to base congregational thinking, priorities, planning, and action.

2. Remarks by Paul C. O'Brien, chairman of New England Telephone, Newcomen Society award ceremony, printed in *The Executive Speaker*, February 1995.

EVERYTHING CHANGED AT ST THOMAS' WHEN THE LEADERS REALIZED THE VALUE OF THEIR DEMOGRAPHIC PROFILE TO LOCAL ADVERTISERS.

CHAPTER 2

How to Identify a Worshiper

In 1934 Roger Tory Peterson developed the "Peterson System" to identify live birds from a distance. Peterson's precise drawings and schematic illustrations replaced the shotgun as the primary tool for discovering the unique field marks of each species. What are field marks? For birds, field marks are their "trademarks of nature"—color, tail and wing patterns, and rump patches—distinguishing one species from another. What are the field marks of worshipers? What specific features tag their common nature? Just as bird-watchers rely on accurate drawings, the following field marks of congregations and their worshipers can instruct serious observers of American religious life.

Who Worships Where?

People who attend religious services in a church, synagogue, or temple exhibit unique traits. These worshipers differ from the average American in several ways. What are their field marks?[1]

---

1. All figures for worshipers and congregations are from the second wave of the U.S. Congregational Life Survey, conducted in the fall of 2008 and the spring of 2009. For more detail about how we surveyed worshipers across America, see appendix 1. All percentages are rounded to the nearest whole number. As a result, responses for some questions will total 99% or 101%. This is a standard convention in social scientific survey reporting. For

Men or women? There are fewer men (39%) in worship than women (61%). Since the U.S. Census Bureau reports that 51% of the U.S. population is female, this means women are more often drawn to congregational life than men. In fact, there are more women than men in the pews in every age category. Among worshipers over 65 years of age, women account for 63%. Of course, this is partly because women live longer than

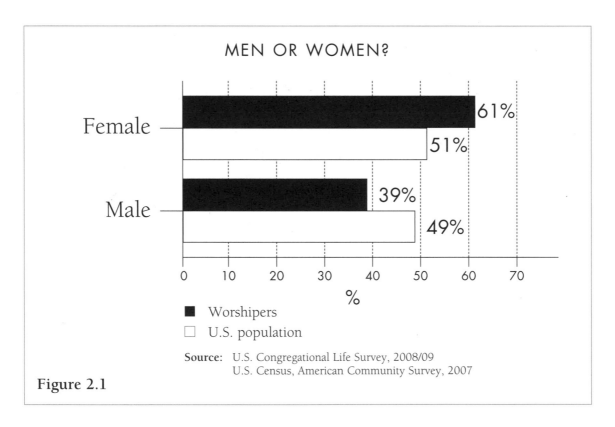

Figure 2.1

questions that allowed more than one response, percentages may total more than 100%. Because the survey was completed by worshipers 15 years of age and older, all the statistics in the book refer only to people in that age group unless otherwise specified. For example, if the text says 50% of worshipers have a particular trait, it means that 50% of all worshipers 15 and older have that characteristic. It tells us nothing about the common features of worshipers less than 15 years of age. In the same way, to make comparisons between worshipers and the American population, information presented from the U.S. Census also refers only to Americans 15 years of age and older.

men by an average of 5 years. The smallest gender gap between worshipers is among people between 15 and 24 years of age. In this age group, the percentage of female worshipers exceeds male worshipers by only 14%. (See Figure 2.1.)

How old are they? The average age of a worshiper is 54 years. (Remember: We're only talking about the average age of those 15 years of age and older.) The average age of the country's over-15 population is only 44 years. Thus, the average worshiper is 10 years older than the average American. Among worshipers, those between the ages of 45 and 64 (39%) are the biggest age group. (See Figure 2.2.)

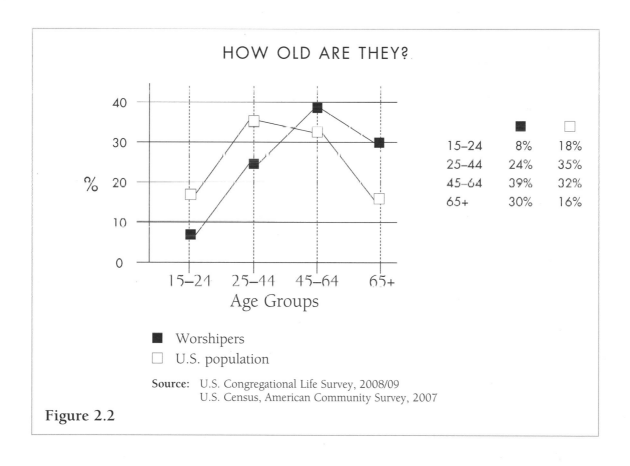

Figure 2.2

Do they work outside the home? Half of all worshipers (59%) are employed full- or part-time. Compared to the U.S. population, worshipers are more likely to be retired. In fact, three in ten worshipers (29%) are retired, which is much higher than the average of 14% for all Americans. Obviously, the larger percentage of retired worshipers is related to the large percentage of older worshipers. Fewer than one in ten worshipers (8%) describe themselves as homemakers. Students make up 7% of all worshipers.[2]

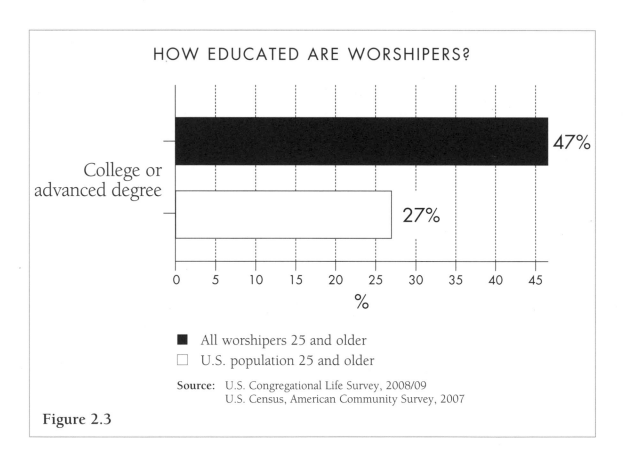

Figure 2.3

2. Employment figures are calculated for worshipers 16 years of age and older because the U.S. Census reports employment for persons 16 years of age and older. The percentage of worshipers who are students is calculated for worshipers 15 years of age and older.

How much education do they have? Worshipers in the U.S. tend to be well educated. The U.S. Census reports that across the country about 27% of the population has a college degree or higher education. The Census reports this figure for people 25 years of age or older. Among worshipers 25 years of age or older, the figure is 47%. This percentage climbs to 53% for attendees less than 65 years of age. Fully 95% of all worshipers have completed high school.[3] (See Figure 2.3.)

What is their annual income? People in the pews come from all walks of life. One in five worshipers are in households that earn less than $25,000 a year. One in four earn

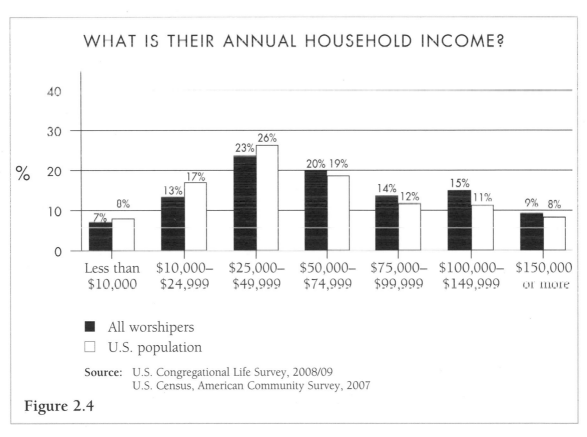

WHAT IS THEIR ANNUAL HOUSEHOLD INCOME?

■ All worshipers
☐ U.S. population

Source: U.S. Congregational Life Survey, 2008/09
U.S. Census, American Community Survey, 2007

Figure 2.4

3. U.S. Census, American Community Survey, 2007.

between $25,000 and $50,000 a year, with another one in four earning $100,000 or more a year. Only 7% earn less than $10,000 a year. The U.S. Census reports the median household income is $50,740. Among worshipers, the average is $62,500. (See Figure 2.4.)

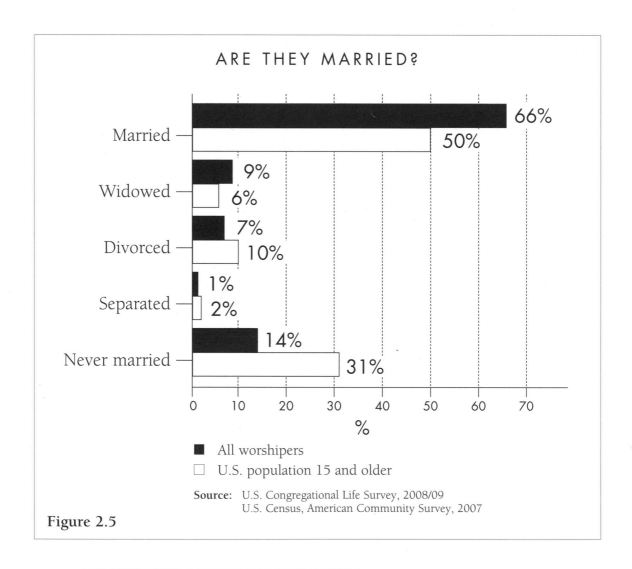

ARE THEY MARRIED?

Married — 66% / 50%
Widowed — 9% / 6%
Divorced — 7% / 10%
Separated — 1% / 2%
Never married — 14% / 31%

■ All worshipers
☐ U.S. population 15 and older

Source: U.S. Congregational Life Survey, 2008/09
U.S. Census, American Community Survey, 2007

Figure 2.5

Are they married? Most worshipers in America are married (66%)—and most of these in their first marriage (54% of all worshipers are in their first marriage). Just over a tenth (12%) have remarried after divorce or the death of a spouse. Congregational participants are therefore much more likely to be married than the average person (50% of the U.S. population are married). Only 8% of worshipers are separated or divorced, compared to a national figure of 13%. A small number of attendees (3%) are living together in a committed relationship other than marriage. The largest group of single people in congregational life consists of those who have never been married. They make up 14% of people in the pews. (See Figure 2.5.)

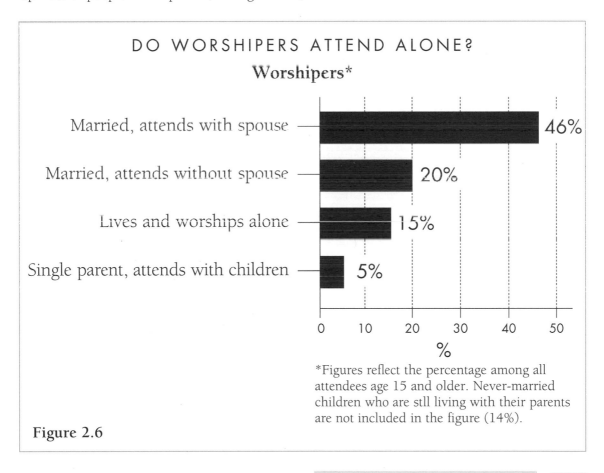

DO WORSHIPERS ATTEND ALONE?

Worshipers*

Married, attends with spouse	46%
Married, attends without spouse	20%
Lives and worships alone	15%
Single parent, attends with children	5%

%

*Figures reflect the percentage among all attendees age 15 and older. Never-married children who are stll living with their parents are not included in the figure (14%).

Figure 2.6

Do worshipers attend services alone? Half of the people who completed the survey during worship services said they were attending with their spouse or partner. But not all married adults attend services with their spouse—about one in five attend without their spouse. (See Figure 2.6.)

Do they have children? Another area of dramatic difference between worshipers and the general public relates to children in the home. People with kids are more likely to go to church or to religious services. Two out of five worshipers (43%) have children living at home. In the U.S. population, the comparable percentage is only 34%. The average worshiper with children living at home has two children. The second-largest household type among worshipers (41%) is adults, whether married or unrelated, living together without children. About 15% of worshipers live alone. Others are single parents attending with their children (5%).

What is their race and ethnicity? Worshipers are similar to other Americans in terms of the proportion who are white, Hispanic, or Asian. More than three out of four worshipers (81%) are white (compared to 76% of the U.S. population).[4] Hispanics (10%) were the second-largest ethnic group in the study (compared to 15% in the U.S. population). Four percent of worshipers are Asian, less than the percentage in the general population. While 13% of the U.S. population are African Americans, only 5% of the surveys were completed by African American worshipers.[5]

---

4. The U.S. population percentages in this paragraph were adjusted for the population 15 years of age and older.

5. Historically black denomination churches (e.g., African Methodist Episcopal, National Baptist) and congregations of faith groups with large percentages of black worshipers (e.g., Muslim masjids, predominantly African American Catholic parishes) are underrepresented in the U.S. Congregational Life Survey. The results of a parallel study describing black religious communities are found in Stephen C. Rasor and Christine D. Chapman, *Black Power from the Pew* (Cleveland, OH: Pilgrim Press, 2007).

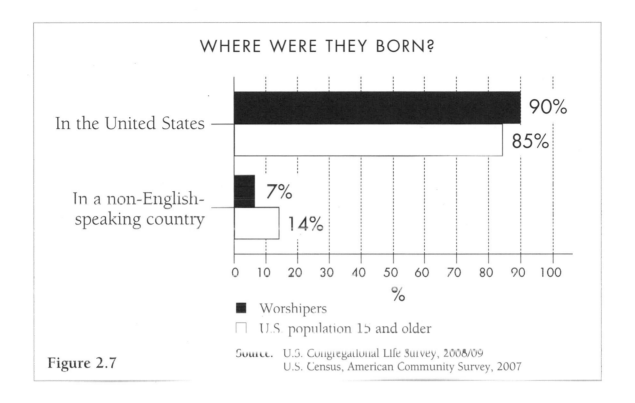

WHERE WERE THEY BORN?

In the United States — 90% / 85%

In a non-English-speaking country — 7% / 14%

0 10 20 30 40 50 60 70 80 90 100
%

■ Worshipers
□ U.S. population 15 and older

Source. U.S. Congregational Life Survey, 2008/09
U.S. Census, American Community Survey, 2007

Figure 2.7

Where were they born? Throughout American history, new immigrant groups have found their place of worship to be a source of support in a new country. Their congregations and parishes provided a place where native languages and customs could be continued and networks of families and friends maintained. One in ten worshipers were *not* born in the United States. This compares to 15% of people living in the United States who were foreign born. The majority of foreign-born worshipers (70%) were born in non-English-speaking countries. Few worshipers (14%) are second-generation Americans—with both parents born outside the United States. For almost all worshipers (89%), English is their first language.[6]

6. As noted above, the U.S. Congregational Life Survey underrepresents congregations with large percentages of immigrant worshipers, especially those with non-English-speaking worshipers. Surveys were available in Spanish and Korean, but few congregations requested them.

Location, location, location. The trip to worship is a short one. Six out of ten worshipers (56%) can get to religious services in just 10 minutes or less. Almost all (90%) can get to their congregation's site in 20 minutes or less. The worshiper who travels 30 minutes or more is a rare person. Only 3% of the participants travel for more than half an hour to attend services. In contrast, the U.S. Census shows that people spend an average of 24 minutes to get to work.[7]

What Matters?

The field marks illustrated in this chapter help leaders and others begin to identify the unique characteristics of their worshipers. People who worship together differ from other Americans in profound ways. Worshipers are more educated, with large percentages holding college degrees. More women than men participate in congregational life. Congregations draw greater percentages of married adults and households with children. Whites and the middle class more often attend services than the poor or racial-ethnic minorities.

The distinctive demographics of American worshipers plant a foundation for human or social capital. Congregations—groups of bonded individuals—are a ready resource in today's world. Because of who worshipers are, they are well prepared to help each other and aid their local communities. Scholars describe how worshiping com-

7. U.S. Census, American Community Survey, 2003.

munities changed America by initiating social welfare projects (e.g., food programs for the hungry), fostering political activities and social movements (e.g., civil rights movements), operating as a mechanism for retaining racial and ethnic community identity, and solidifying cultural expressions.[8] That powerful potential remains.

8. Roger Finke and Rodney Stark, *The Churching of America, 1776–2005: Winners and Losers in Our Religious Economy* (New Brunswick, NJ: Rutgers University Press, 2005), and Mark Chaves, *Congregations in America* (Cambridge, MA: Harvard University Press, 2004).

CHAPTER 3

HOW TO IDENTIFY A CONGREGATION

Many voluntary organizations flourish in America, from the Rotary Club to book clubs, from intramural sports teams to professional organizations, from neighborhood home-owners' associations to sororities and fraternities. Responses from 5,000 congregations that participated in the survey told us a lot that helps distinguish them from other voluntary organizations.

How large? Congregational size can be determined in several ways [1] The largest figures were reported when we asked about the total number of people associated *in any way* with the congregation—this includes adults and children, members and nonmembers, regular participants and infrequent attendees. The average (median) congregation or parish size using this yardstick was 277. Looking at people who *regularly* participate in the congregation reduces the average to 130. Further restricting the view to worshipers older than age 18 who regularly participate brings the average down to 85. We also asked about the average attendance in worship (which would often include teenagers

---

1. The results in this chapter come from a congregational profile completed by one leader in each congregation rather than from individual worshipers' responses. The profile provided information about the facilities, programs, finances, and staff of each congregation.

HOW LARGE ARE U.S. CONGREGATIONS?

	Median
Number of people associated in any way with the congregation	277
Number of people regularly participating in the congregation	130
Number of adults (18 and up) regularly participating in the congregation	85
Average worship attendance	95

Figure 3.1

and children) and found an average of 95 people. Typically, Catholic parishes are far larger than Protestant churches and other kinds of congregations. (See Figure 3.1.)

What is the congregation's affiliation? Most congregations (92%) cite an affiliation with a denomination, convention, or other association. Methodist churches make up the largest group (17% of affiliated congregations in the national sample, almost all of which are part of the United Methodist Church). Other denominational groups with many participating congregations include Roman Catholic parishes (13%), Baptist churches (14% of affiliated churches, including 5% affiliated with the American Baptists and 6% with the Southern Baptist Convention), and Lutheran churches (13% overall, including 11% that are affiliated with the Evangelical Lutheran Church in America). A wide variety of denominations are included in the study, from Mennonites to Unitarians, from Reform Jews to Quakers. (See Figure 3.2 for denominational groups; appendix 3 provides the complete list of denominations.)

Where does the congregation worship? Almost all congregations and parishes (99%) hold their primary worship service in a church, synagogue, or temple—not surprising, given the affiliation of participating congregations. Others worship in school buildings, theaters, shopping malls, and community centers. Most own their own facilities (97%). The remainder rent space or meet for free in a building owned by oth-

FROM WHAT FAITH GROUPS DO CONGREGATIONS COME?*

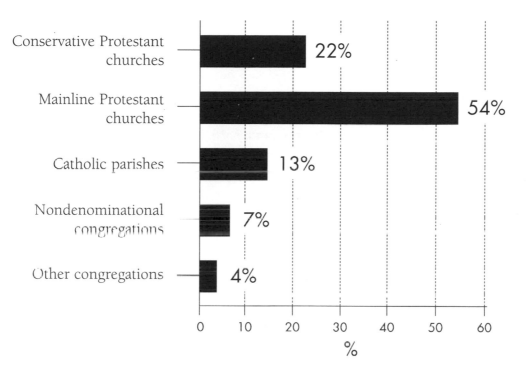

*The classifications represent faith groups as typically defined in sociological research. Mainline Protestant traditions include denominations that are affiliated with the National Council of Churches; conservative Protestant groups include evangelical and Pentecostal denominations. Nondenominational congregations are not affiliated with any national body. Other congregations are non-Christian congregations.

Figure 3.2

ers. On average, the space where a congregation's largest worship service is held seats almost 250 people, but the range of sizes is impressive—the smallest space seats 75 and the largest seats more than 3,000. Most congregations (96%) have services in only one location.

Do others in the community use the building? Many congregations share their building and facilities with community groups not connected to the congregation. About half (46%) of congregations have other groups in their building on at least a weekly basis. Yet one in ten never share their facilities with others in the community.

How is the congregation financially supported? All congregations and parishes list individual contributions (in the form of offerings, pledges, donations, or dues) as one of the three biggest sources of income. One-third also cite income from trust funds, investments, or bequests. Another one in four (25%) report income from charges for use of the congregation's facilities or buildings.

The median congregational income from all sources is about $210,450 annually and ranges from somewhat less than $50,000 to a high of more than $5 million. Congregational expenses (including salaries, debt service, money sent to the denomination or other religious organizations, and all other costs) average $15,430 more than the average congregation's income. Operating expenses alone average about $167,000 annually. Thus, the typical congregation spends most of its income on day-to-day operating expenses and a much smaller portion on other activities and mission programs. (See Figure 3.3.)

When asked to describe the congregation's financial situation, more than half (57%) reported that the congregation has an essentially stable financial base, and only 12% enjoy an increasing financial base. The remaining congregations are not so fortunate—one in three (29%) overall have a declining base, and 1% face a financial situation

> ## FAST FACT
>
> ### Congregations change their worship services to attract new people.
>
> *In the previous five years, 22% of congregations started a new service, 18% changed an existing service, and of these, 8% did both. By adapting their worship offerings, these congregations seek to meet the needs of current and prospective members.*

HOW IS THE CONGREGATION FINANCIALLY SUPPORTED?

	Median Amount for Most Recent Fiscal Year
Income from all sources	$210,450
Income from individuals' donations	$167,105
Total congregation budget	$225,880
Congregation's operating expenses	$160,000

Figure 3.3

that is a serious threat to their continued existence. Yet only half of all congregations report that they conduct an annual financial stewardship campaign.

How is the congregation staffed? All but 3% of congregations have at least some paid staff. Most (85%) have at least one full-time ordained professional staff person, and 68% have just one such person on staff. Some congregations employ nonordained pastoral leaders or other lay ministers—one in four congregations have at least one such full-time professional on staff. Other categories of full-time employees (for example, clerical or custodial) are also reported by about a third of congregations (29%). (See Figure 3.4.)

How old is the congregation? Few participating congregations were founded recently—just 6% were established in the last 20 years. Rather, many have stood the test of time—one-half are more than 100 years old, and the median age is 94 years.

How are congregations changing? In the past five years about 6% of congregations changed their name. While this percentage appears small, this means on a national level an estimated 3,960 congregations change their name in a typical year.[2]

2. This statistic is based on an estimate of 330,000 congregations in the United States.

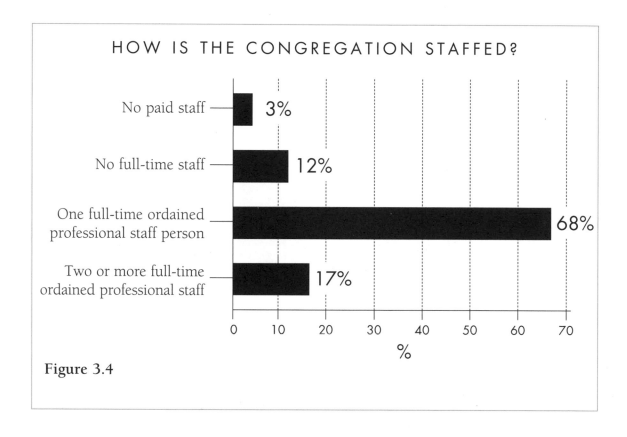

HOW IS THE CONGREGATION STAFFED?

No paid staff — 3%

No full-time staff — 12%

One full-time ordained professional staff person — 68%

Two or more full-time ordained professional staff — 17%

0   10   20   30   40   50   60   70

%

Figure 3.4

Sometimes congregations move to a new location (4% reported making such a change in the past five years). Again, even this small percentage translates into 2,640 congregations moving in an average year. (See Figure 3.5.)

Half of congregations report that worship attendance has declined in the past five years (49% report more than a 5% drop in attendance between 2003 and 2008). About one in five report worship attendance has grown more than 5% in that same time period (slightly more common among Catholic parishes than among Protestant and other congregations). About one in three (29%) have experienced stable worship attendance (attendance that changed by less than 5%) in the past five years. (See Figure 3.6.)

HOW HAS THE CONGREGATION CHANGED?

In the past five years the congregation has . . .

		Estimated Number of Congregations Nationwide	
		In 5 years	In 1 year
Changed its name..	6%	19,800	3,960
Moved to a new location	4%	13,200	2,640
Absorbed another congregation, which closed	1%	3,300	660
Merged with another congregation............................	2%	6,600	1,320
Left a denomination and become independent..........	4%	13,200	2,640
Changed denominations...	1%	3,300	660

Figure 3.5

What Does Typical Mean?

Why does Allison, who attends a megachurch of 5,000 with multiple weekend services, find the preceding description of congregational life hard to believe? Why does Keith, who participates in a mainline Protestant congregation of 350, also wonder why the illustrations in this chapter do not match his experiences? The answer: Allison and Keith, as *typical worshipers*, find themselves in congregations of larger-than-average size. A wide gap exists between where the largest numbers of people worship and the size of the typical congregation. Most congregations are small. But most worshipers are in large congregations.

IS THE CONGREGATION GROWING?*

In the past five years the congregation has experienced . . .

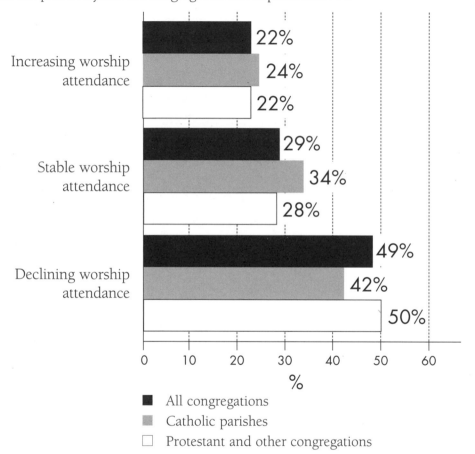

Increasing worship attendance
- 22%
- 24%
- 22%

Stable worship attendance
- 29%
- 34%
- 28%

Declining worship attendance
- 49%
- 42%
- 50%

■ All congregations
▨ Catholic parishes
☐ Protestant and other congregations

*Average worship attendance reported in 2008 minus average worship attendance reported in 2001 divided by 2001 average attendance. Congregations growing more than 5% between 2001 and 2008 were designated as "increasing"; congregations experiencing a decline of more than 5% were categorized as "declining"; remaining congregations were placed in the "stable" category.

Figure 3.6

Imagine a small town of 1,000 people. This town has 10 congregations of various faith groups—Catholic, Protestant, and other religions. If all worshipers were equally spread among the congregations, each congregation would have 100 members (assuming everyone in town attends religious services!). But this is not the case. For example, one of the congregations is a Catholic parish. Since Catholics are organized geographically into parishes, all the Catholics in town would go to the Catholic church. Because Catholics make up 25% of the population, 250 people would be attending Mass there. That leaves only 750 people in town

MYTH TRAP

Congregational giving has declined in recent years.

After adjusting for inflation, worshipers' contributions rose from $1,240 per capita in 2001 to $1,500 in 2008. Congregations' annual income from all sources has been growing even faster than individuals' donations.

as potential worshipers for the other nine congregations. Are the 750 people spread out evenly among the remaining nine congregations? Probably not. One congregation may have a charismatic leader, a wonderful program for children and youth, or a new building. They average 350 people in worship every week. Quite a crowd in this small town! Now only 400 people are left to attend services at the other eight congregations. If each of these eight congregations got their "fair share," it would mean they attract only 50 worshipers each! While eight out of the ten *congregations* are small, the other reality is that 60% of the *people* in this imaginary town worship in a large church, synagogue, or temple.

How do these factors play out in communities across America? Some congregations enjoy a large attendance at their services because of their faith tradition, their exemplary services or programs, or other features. Thus, the *typical* worshiper experiences a large congregation. This does not change the fact that the average congregation has about 100 people in worship.

Explaining the gap between what typical congregations look like and what typical worshipers experience is difficult. As our mythical town illustrates, the distribution of congregations is vastly different from the spread of worshipers across those congregations. A parallel example might be where typical dollars are found. The typical dollar belongs to a wealthy household, but the typical household has few dollars!

Another way to summarize this gap is with the following facts: 10% of U.S. congregations draw 50% of all worshipers each week. Another 40% of congregations have 39% of worshipers attending services that week. The remaining 50% of all congregations have only 11% of the total number of worshipers in a given week.

Finally, unlike the imaginary town, not all Americans associate with a faith community or congregation. Only 63% of the population is claimed by a denomination or faith group, a statistic than has remained stable since 1980.[3] Further, less than 22% of the population report attending worship services each week.[4] Small congregations or congregations of any size in any community will find many people who do not regularly attend worship services.

What Matters?

Much about U.S. congregations and parishes is determined by their key characteristics—affiliation, size, and resource base. Congregations are not evenly distributed across the various faith groups. This means that in a given community there may be several congregations of one faith group (e.g., conservative Protestant) but no congregations representing other types. Some small denominations or faith groups have limited resources to start new congregations or to support struggling existing ones. The number of congregations associated with a denomination or faith group directly affects worshipers who move to a new community hoping to find a congregation like the one they left. If the denomination is small, their new community may not have a congregation of their faith tradition.

3. Roger Finke and Rodney Stark, *The Churching of America 1776–2005: Winners and Losers in Our Religious Economy* (New Brunswick, NJ: Rutgers University Press, 2005), 23. See also *Religious Congregations and Membership in the United States 2000: An Enumeration by Region, State and County Based on Data Reported by 149 Religious Bodies* (Nashville, TN: Glenmary Research Center, 2002).

4. C. Kirk Hadaway and Penny Long Marler, "How Many Americans Attend Worship Each Week? An Alternative Approach to Measurement," *Journal for the Scientific Study of Religion* 44, no. 3 (2005): 307–22.

Most congregations have fewer than 100 people in worship services. This key fact of congregational life has far-reaching consequences. With so few people, raising funds and supporting full-time clergy or other professional staff can pose problems. Most congregations and parishes also own their own building. Again, with fewer than 100 people to fund the upkeep and operational expenses of their facilities, resources are taxed. Day-to-day operating expenses may leave little money to fund extensive programs, capital improvements, community services, or other ministry projects.

A considerable gap often exists between the number of members in a congregation and the number of people who regularly attend services. Worship attendance figures tend to give a more realistic picture of the actual community life and resource base of a congregation. Typically, worship attendance on any given day is about 50% of the membership. All too often congregations have their identity "fixed" on the size of their membership rather than on the number of worshipers. The larger this perception gap is for a congregation, the more likely it is that it needs a new prescription to focus on a new direction.

©hris Morgan www.cxmedia.com

CHAPTER 4

SPIRITUAL CONNECTIONS

The next three chapters of this field guide describe several conceptual building blocks for understanding the complex nature of congregational life: spiritual connections, inside connections, and outside connections. The complexity of these connections illustrates a key lesson from research: congregational life is rarely about one or two variables. Because these dimensions of congregational life are interrelated, dynamics in one place will directly affect all other areas. Where is the best place to begin? Since congregations and parishes primarily focus on worshipers' encounters with God and the sacred, spiritual connections are explored first in this chapter.

What Are Spiritual Connections?

Congregations cultivate faith development and respond to the religious needs of worshipers. Spiritual growth for individual worshipers can result from private devotional activities, participation in worship services or other congregational activities, or participation in activities of other groups or organizations. The spiritual lives of worshipers and the worship activities of their congregations are described below.

Private devotions: How often do worshipers pray, meditate, or read the Bible?
The majority of worshipers (67%) spend at least a few times a week in such activities. A
large percentage (48%) spend time *every day* in prayer, meditation, reading the Bible, or
other private, devotional activities. (See Figure 4.1.)

Growing in faith? Half of all worshipers (49%) say they have experienced much
growth in their faith during the last year. What fostered their growth in faith? One in
three (31%) attribute their spiritual growth to their participation in the congregation,
12% attribute it to their own private activities, and only a few (6%) attribute it to their
involvement in other groups or congregations. Surprisingly, half report that they either
had experienced only some growth in faith (43%) or had not grown in their faith in the
last year (8%). Catholic worshipers are less likely to credit their parish involvement as

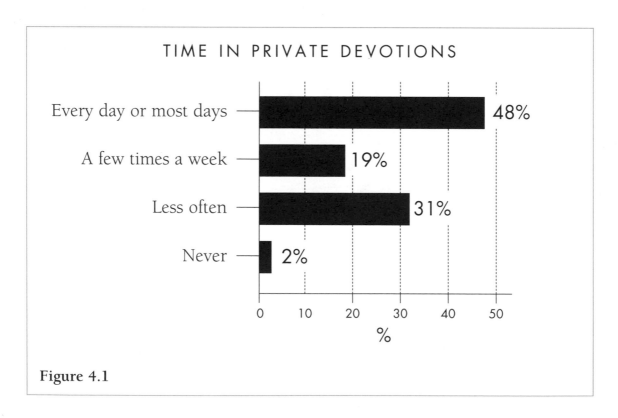

Figure 4.1

A FIELD GUIDE TO U.S. CONGREGATIONS

the source of their spiritual growth and somewhat more likely to credit their personal activities. (See Figure 4.2.)

Rating the congregation or parish: Is it meeting worshipers' spiritual needs? Worshipers give their congregations high marks for meeting their spiritual needs. The majority (85%) believe their spiritual needs are being met through their congregation or parish.

Another sign of satisfaction. Almost all rate the worship services or congregational activities as helpful to everyday living: 56% say their congregation or parish helps them with their daily living "to a great extent," and another 32% say "to some extent."

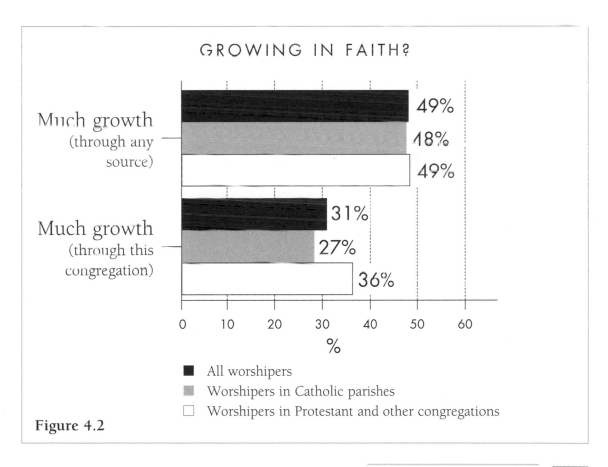

Figure 4.2

Conversion or not? Among all worshipers, about half (47%) report they have had a conversion experience or moment of decisive faith commitment. Worshipers in Protestant churches and congregations of other faith groups are more likely to cite a definite moment of commitment or a conversion experience (53%) than those in Catholic parishes (42%). Surprising percentages of worshipers (Catholics, 26%; Protestants, 21%) are not sure if they have had this type of religious experience. (See Figure 4.3.)

One Book but many views: Views of the Bible. Differing views about the Bible underlie many theological and denominational policy debates. Worshipers were presented with six general statements about the Bible. The statement most often identified by worshipers (49%) as representing their own views was "The Bible is the Word of God, to be interpreted in the light of its historical context and the church's teachings." One-quarter of all worshipers (24%) embrace a more literal understanding of the Bible ("The Bible is the Word of God, to be taken literally word for word"). Fewer than one in five (18%) chose the statement that reflects a mainline Protestant view of the Bible ("The Bible is the Word of God, to be interpreted in the light of its historical and cultural context"). About 6% do not recognize the Bible as the Word of God. Some (3%) confessed that they don't know how they view the Bible. (See Figure 4.4.)

Two distinct views of the Bible emerge when comparing worshipers in Catholic parishes to other worshipers. The majority in Catholic parishes (58%) agreed with the following statement about the Bible: "The Bible is the Word of God, to be interpreted in the light of its historical context and the church's teachings." Non-Catholic worshipers were split—40% agreed with the majority of Catholics, and 31% identified with a literal interpretation of the sacred text: "The Bible is the Word of God, to be taken literally word for word."

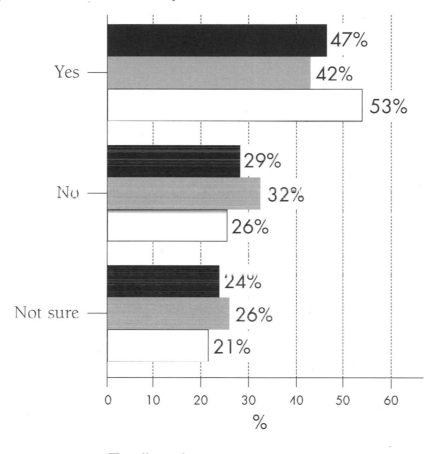

CONVERSION OR NOT?

Have you ever had a conversion experience or a moment of decisive faith commitment?

- All worshipers
- Worshipers in Catholic parishes
- Worshipers in Protestant and other congregations

Figure 4.3

How do worshipers view God's nature? Views about God and Jesus. Most worshipers believe God is directly involved in worldly affairs (76%). Fewer believe God is angered by human sin (64%). Combining these two dimensions provides four views of God:

- an authoritarian God who is angry and involved in worldly affairs
- a benevolent God who is involved in the world but not angry
- a critical God who is angry but not involved in worldly affairs
- a distant God who is not angry and is not involved in the world[1]

A majority of worshipers (53%) hold an authoritarian view of God. (See Figure 4.5.)

VIEWS OF THE BIBLE

Which statement comes closest to your view of the Bible? (Mark only *one*.)

The Bible is the Word of God, to be taken literally word for word 24%

The Bible is the Word of God, to be interpreted in the light of its
historical context and the church's teachings 49%

The Bible is the Word of God, to be interpreted in the light of its
historical and cultural context 18%

The Bible is not the Word of God, but contains God's Word to us 4%

The Bible is not the Word of God, but is a valuable book 2%

The Bible is an ancient book with little value today .... *

Don't know 3%

* Fewer than 1% of worshipers chose this response.

Figure 4.4

---

1. Paul Froese and Christopher D. Bader, "God in America: Why Theology Is Not Simply the Concern of Philosophers," *Journal for the Scientific Study of Religion* 46 (2007): 465–81.

The worshiping community is almost evenly split between those who view Jesus as the only path to salvation (45%) and those who are open to other paths to salvation (37%). About one in five attendees just aren't sure (18%) about the criteria for salvation.

"I like mine, but they're all good." Half of all worshipers take a relativist stance toward religion—that is, they believe "all the different religions are equally good ways of helping a person find ultimate truth." Almost one-third (29%) disagreed with this statement, and 20% were neutral or unsure about it.

How do people experience the worship services of their congregation? Most say they feel a sense of God's presence during worship and experience joy and inspiration. Some report that they gain a sense of fulfilling their obligations by attending worship. It is less common for people to say they experience awe, mystery, or spontaneity as they

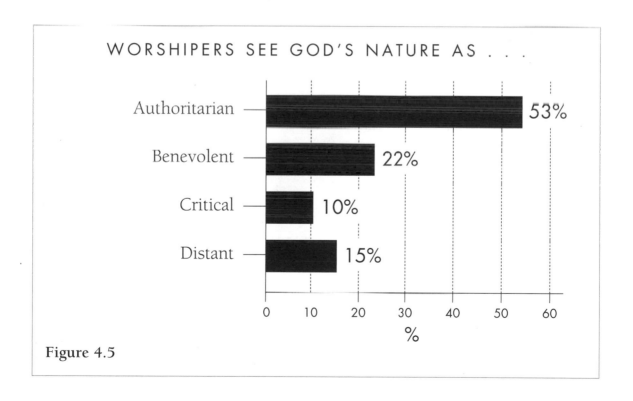

Figure 4.5

worship. Thankfully, most people do not have a negative experience, such as boredom or frustration. (See Figure 4.6.)

Hymns top the charts. The majority of worshipers (56%) prefer traditional hymns

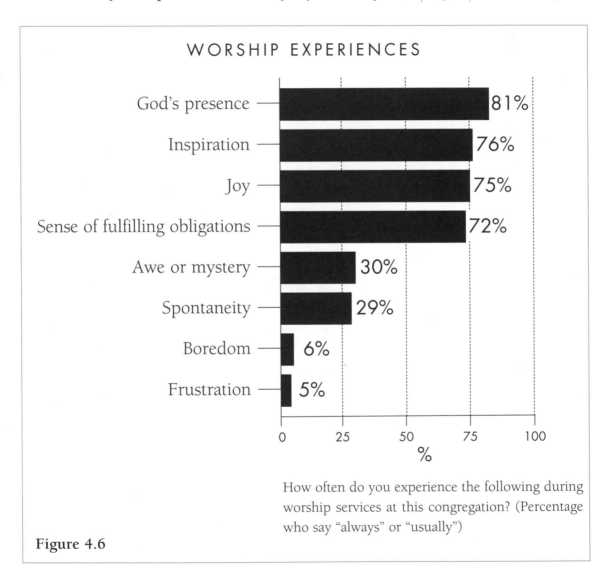

WORSHIP EXPERIENCES

How often do you experience the following during worship services at this congregation? (Percentage who say "always" or "usually")

Figure 4.6

over other styles of music during congregational worship. One in three (31%) prefer praise music or choruses, and 26% prefer contemporary hymns. (Note: Worshipers could choose up to two styles of music.) Other styles of music are preferred by fewer people—contemporary music other than hymns (15%), gospel (15%), music or songs from a variety of cultures (9%), classical music (9%), sung responsorial psalms (8%), and contemplative chants (2%). (See Figure 4.7.)

HYMNS TOP THE CHARTS

While you may value many different styles of music, which of the following do you prefer in congregational worship? (Mark up to *two* options.)

Traditional hymns	56%
Praise music or choruses	31%
Contemporary hymns	26%
Other contemporary music or songs (not hymns)	15%
Gospel music	15%
Music or songs from a variety of cultures	9%
Classical music or chorales	9%
Sung responsorial psalms	8%
Contemplative chants (Taizé, Iona)	2%
No music or songs	2%
Don't know	3%

Figure 4.7

Worship as the Main Event

The spiritual lives of attendees are further enriched by their experiences with others in worship. What are congregations offering to participants? How do congregations organize these regular opportunities to experience the sacred?

When and how many services? It's no longer just a once-a-week Sunday morning affair, and for some faith traditions it never was! *One-half* of congregations offer more than one worship service in a typical week. These services may be on Saturday or Friday or Monday, but most are on Sunday. Of course, some faith traditions have had a history of more than one Sunday worship service. For example, Southern Baptists traditionally had a morning service as well as an evening service, and faithful worshipers were expected to attend both. Many congregations, however, have abandoned this practice. Multiple services, especially over a weekend, are often offered to give worshipers a convenient choice of worship times. Roman Catholics have long had these options since, in many parishes, Mass is offered daily and a number of times on weekends. Furthermore, Saturday is the sacred day for worship for Seventh-day Adventists and Jews.

We asked congregations to give us specific information for up to five worship services. In all, they told us about hundreds of different services. Four in five of these services are held on Sunday. Wednesday and Saturday are also common days for services—9% of services take place on Wednesday and 8% on Saturday.

Most of these services occur weekly (96%), but others are seasonal (for example, services held on Good Friday or other holy days) or periodic (biweekly or monthly). The largest percentage of services (17%) start at 11:00 a.m., and slightly more than half (55%) start in the period between 9:00 and 11:00 a.m. Only 16% start at 6:00 p.m. or later.

Slightly more than half of these services were described as traditional in style, 16% as contemporary, and 28% as blended. One-quarter (26%) are for nonmembers or "seekers," those searching for a new faith community.

These patterns reflect the changes congregations have made in the past five years to expand their worship service offerings. One in five (22%) have started a new worship service—sometimes targeting a new group that they were not reaching before (7% did so). Even without adding more services, one in five changed the style of their worship service in the past five years.

What happens in the typical worship service? In almost all worship services, someone preaches a sermon or homily or gives a speech or talk. The sermon, homily, or speech usually lasts between 11 and 20 minutes, although some worshipers enjoy a stirring hour's worth or more.

Most congregations take an offering or collect money during worship services. Because individual contributions are the major source of income for most congregations, this is a key element.

MYTH TRAP
Most worshipers prefer traditional hymns.

Musical preferences are related to age. While two out of three worshipers 40 years of age and older prefer traditional hymns, less than half of those under 40 prefer traditional hymns. And our findings say nothing about the musical preferences of people who are not currently attending worship services.

Music finds its way into worship services in a variety of ways. In most services, worshipers hear singing in unison by the congregation and by choirs or soloists who perform music. Pianos or organs accompany the service more often than drums or electric guitar.

Communion, the Eucharist, or Lord's Supper is often observed in worship. (See Figure 4.8.)

What kind of music? Traditional hymns are still the most common type of music in most services. Almost all congregations (95%) include traditional hymns in their largest worship service. More than half of congregations include both contemporary hymns (58%) and praise music or choruses (54%) in their largest service. Responsive psalms are common in Catholic parishes but are also used in non-Catholic settings—one-quarter of congregations overall use such music.

This pattern—traditional hymns as most common, followed by contemporary hymns and praise music—mirrors what worshipers say they prefer. Congregations appear to be responding to the music preferences of their worshipers. But whether the

THE LARGEST (OR ONLY) WORSHIP SERVICE INCLUDES*:

Sermon, homily, or speech	100%
Singing by the congregation	98%
Taking up a collection of money	96%
Use of amplification equipment	87%
People greeting one another	83%
Length between 1 and 1½ hours	83%
Piano	83%
Singing by a choir or soloist	74%
Hymnbooks	74%
Communion, Eucharist, Lord's Supper	72%
People speaking, reading, or reciting something together	66%
Organ	66%
Laughter	66%
Special time directed at children	65%
Written bulletin or service outline	60%
Silent prayer or meditation	57%
Leader wears robe or other special garments	56%

*Only those cited by a majority of congregations are shown.

Figure 4.8

musical offerings address the preferences of those outside the faith community who are searching for a new congregation or underrepresented groups within the congregation—younger generations, in particular—is unknown.

What Matters?

For most participants in U.S. congregations, worship is the main event. While some participate in small groups within the congregation or serve the community through the congregation (described in the following chapter), the majority experience the congregation only by attending worship services. Thus, what they get from their religious community must happen during worship. The results here suggest that tremendous care, attention, and planning should be directed at the worship service. Many worshipers are finding the services helpful as they seek to navigate their everyday lives. However, a large percentage say that they attend as a way to fulfill an obligation, and some report that their faith is fostered in venues outside the congregation. Half of all worshipers say they are not growing in their faith. How long will they continue to participate in a faith community if this is the case?

THE INTRODUCTION OF INDIVIDUAL TV SCREENS AT ST PAT'S
MEANT THAT EACH PARISIONER NOW HAD THE CHOICE OF
OVER 700 EXCELLENT PREACHERS, 68000 SERMONS,
12000000 WORSHIP SONGS AND 32 VERSIONS OF THE BIBLE.

CHAPTER 5

INSIDE CONNECTIONS

Field guides note and illustrate the behaviors of the species under scrutiny. While the spiritual experiences covered in the previous chapter are subjective and sometimes tough to describe, this chapter begins with a focus on the behaviors of worshipers linked to their congregations. We call these "inside connections." How do worshipers relate to one another? What activities of the congregation are they involved in beyond worship? This second area of congregational life captures worshipers' involvement in small groups and leadership roles, decision making, and financial contributions. Inside connections also entail how worshipers feel about their relationships with other worshipers. For example, do they feel a strong sense of belonging to their congregation? Do they have friends in the congregation?

Worshiper Behavior

This first section describes what attendees actually do in and with their congregation. Some become official members, join groups, become leaders, or make important decisions on behalf of the congregation. In addition to making a commitment of time, many worshipers commit financially by contributing money to the congregation's mission.

Becoming a member. One in ten worshipers regularly participate in the congregation but are not members. Another 2% are in the process of becoming members. The majority (77%) are members.[1]

Involvement in small groups. Less than half of all worshipers (45%) are involved in small groups organized by the congregation. Fellowship groups, clubs, and other social groups associated with the congregation draw the largest group of worshipers (28% overall). Sunday school, church school, or other religious education groups draw 19% of all worshipers. Prayer, discussion, and Bible study groups also draw 19% of all worshipers. (Some worshipers participate in more than one type of group.) But worshipers in Protestant churches and congregations of other faith groups are far more likely to be involved in such groups than worshipers in Catholic parishes. Only 30% of those in Catholic parishes are involved in small-group activities. Worshipers in other types of congregations participate at twice this level—60% relate to some type of small group in their congregation. While worshipers in Catholic parishes report lower levels of involvement with all three types of small groups, the largest gap exists for church or Sunday school (29% of Protestants and others, but only 9% of Catholics). (See Figure 5.1.)

Worshipers as leaders. Four in ten worshipers (40%) serve as leaders in their congregation. These attendees serve on committees, task forces, or the governing board of the congregation; lead or assist in worship; sing in the choir; serve as religious education teachers or church officers; and take on other leadership responsibilities important to congregational life. (See Figure 5.2.)

Again, a large difference exists between worshipers in Catholic parishes and others. Fewer than one in three in Catholic parishes say they hold a leadership position in their parish, while one in two Protestants and others report serving in such a role in their congregation. This large difference results from at least three factors. First, Catholic parishes are large compared to the average size of other congregations. Thus, in Catholic parishes there are simply fewer leadership positions per person in the pew to be filled. Second, the centralized decision-making structure and other polity differences between Catholic parishes and other congregations contribute to a lower number of available

---

1. The remaining 10% of worshipers are not members, but are visitors or infrequent attendees.

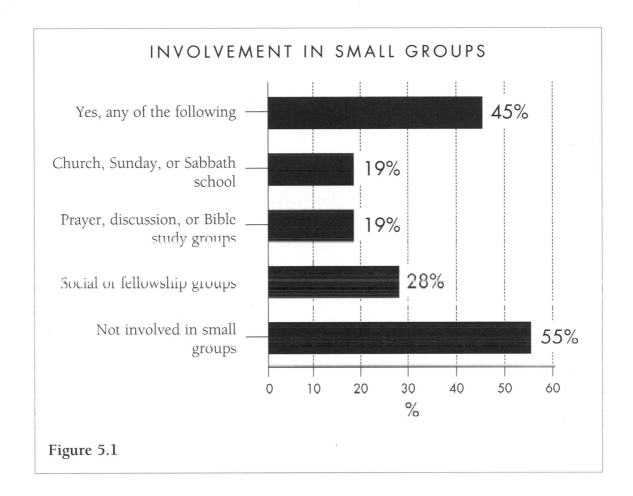

INVOLVEMENT IN SMALL GROUPS

Yes, any of the following — 45%

Church, Sunday, or Sabbath school — 19%

Prayer, discussion, or Bible study groups — 19%

Social or fellowship groups — 28%

Not involved in small groups — 55%

0 10 20 30 40 50 60
%

Figure 5.1

leadership roles. Third, other evidence suggests that in fact Catholic worshipers participate in parish life other than attending Mass at lower rates than other denominations or faith groups.[2]

2. Cynthia Woolever and Deborah Bruce, *Places of Promise* (Louisville, KY: Westminster John Knox Press, 2008), 106; Robert Dixon, "Variation by Age in Parish Involvement Scores of Catholic Church Attenders in Australia, New Zealand and the United States: Age Effect or Generational Effect?" *Journal of Beliefs and Values* 27, no. 1 (2006): 81–82; D. Hoge, W. Dinges, M. Johnson, and J. Gonzales Jr., *Young Adult Catholics: Religion in the Culture of Choice* (Notre Dame, IN: University of Notre Dame Press, 2001), 69.

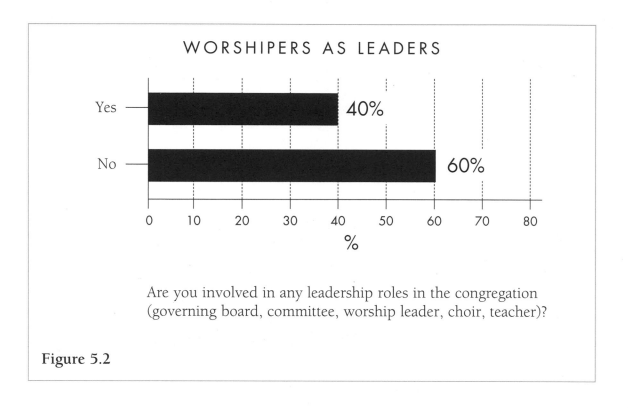

WORSHIPERS AS LEADERS

Are you involved in any leadership roles in the congregation (governing board, committee, worship leader, choir, teacher)?

Figure 5.2

Involved in making decisions. While most worshipers (67%) say they have been given the opportunity to participate in congregational decision making, less than a third (29%) even occasionally do so. More (38%) feel they've been given the opportunity but have chosen not to get involved in important decision making. One-quarter (27%) say they have *not* been given the chance to be decision makers but are happy with the situation as it is. Only 6% expressed any dissatisfaction about not being part of decisions in the congregation.

Worshipers in Catholic parishes are less likely to get involved in decisions affecting parish life. But they are as likely as those in other faith groups to feel they have been given the opportunity to have a say in important decisions.

Participating—for how long? One-third of worshipers are new people who have been attending their current congregation for five years or less. (We'll look at new people in more depth later in this chapter and again in chapter 7.) Another third have been attending there for between 6 and 20 years, and 29% have been participating for more than 20 years. A small number (4%) are visitors to the congregation—including those who usually attend another congregation and those who don't usually attend services anywhere. (See Figure 5.3.)

Participating—more or less? Only a small percentage (14%) of worshipers describe themselves as participating in congregational activities less than they did two years ago. A quarter (25%) boast they are participating more than they did in the past.

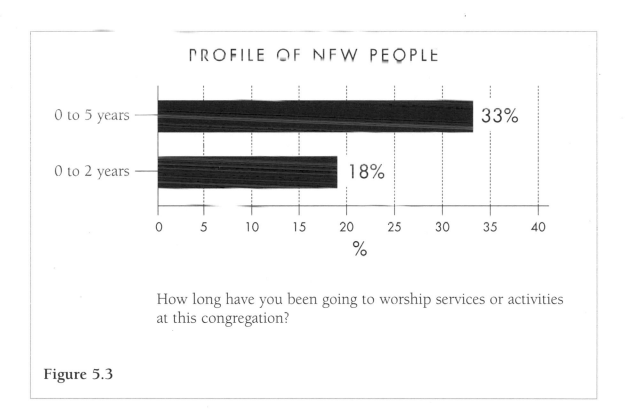

PROFILE OF NEW PEOPLE

0 to 5 years — 33%

0 to 2 years — 18%

How long have you been going to worship services or activities at this congregation?

Figure 5.3

The largest group (51%) depicts their participation as stable, not having changed much in the past two years.

Making financial contributions. Most congregations and parishes heavily depend on worshipers' monetary gifts in order to operate. Worshipers give to their congregations at quite diverse levels, and their level of giving is not associated with their income. In other words, people with large incomes do not necessarily give a higher percentage of their money than worshipers with more limited financial resources.[3] The biblical understanding of tithing—giving 10% or more of earnings to the congregation—is practiced by fewer than one in five worshipers (18%).

However, there is a wide gap in the practice of tithing between Catholics and other worshipers. While one in ten Catholic worshipers tithe, one-fourth of Protestant worshipers are tithers. Compared to others, Catholics are more likely to say they give a small amount whenever they attend Mass (26% vs. 13% for those attending other worship services).

The more common giving practice among the majority of worshipers is to give a smaller percentage on a regular basis (28% give 5% to 9% of their income, and 27% give less than 5% of their income). One in five give only a small amount whenever they attend worship services. A few (7%) never contribute money to the congregation. (See Figure 5.4.)

3. Dean Hoge, Charles Zech, Patrick McNamara, and Michael Donahue, *Money Matters: Personal Giving in American Churches* (Louisville, KY: Westminster John Knox Press, 1996), 58.

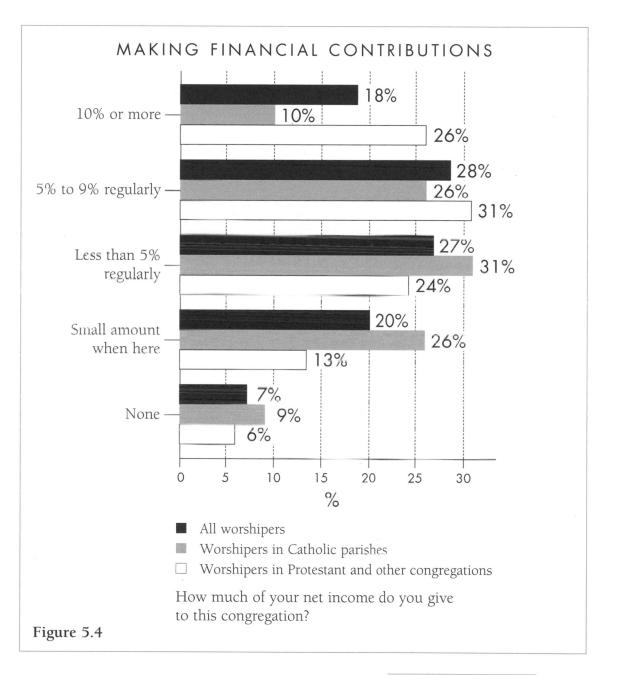

MAKING FINANCIAL CONTRIBUTIONS

10% or more — 18% / 10% / 26%

5% to 9% regularly — 28% / 26% / 31%

Less than 5% regularly — 27% / 31% / 24%

Small amount when here — 20% / 26% / 13%

None — 7% / 9% / 6%

%

■ All worshipers
■ Worshipers in Catholic parishes
□ Worshipers in Protestant and other congregations

How much of your net income do you give
to this congregation?

Figure 5.4

It's All about Relationships

Many worshipers say their congregation or parish is like a family. Using phrases like "my church" or "our parish" connotes a sense of ownership and a close identification with the congregation. Many experts believe these horizontal connections are as important as the vertical connection with God for the congregation's ministry. In the next section, three subjective aspects of congregational relationships are considered—the sense of belonging, having friends in the congregation, and the presence or absence of conflict.

I know I belong here. Congregations receive high marks for making people feel at home. Seven in ten worshipers (71%) have a strong sense of belonging to their congregation. Two out of five worshipers (42%) not only describe a strong sense of belonging but also say this feeling has been growing. Protestants and those from other faith groups are more likely than Catholics to say this sense of belonging is growing.

Some of my best friends go here. Two-thirds (67%) of all worshipers count at least some close friends among the other worshipers in their congregation; only a small percentage (11%) say *all* of their close friends attend there. A significant minority (15%) indicate that they have little contact with others from the congregation outside of scheduled activities, and 18% have some friends in their congregation but say their closest friends don't attend there.

What about conflict? Like families, people in congregations do not always agree. How much conflict is there in congregations or, more accurately, how much are worshipers aware of disagreements? Almost half of all worshipers (47%) said that there had been no conflict in their congregation over the past two years. But another one in four observed "some conflict."

FAST FACT

One in ten worshipers who regularly attend are *not* members of the congregation.

This percentage is twice as high among worshipers under the age of 25 (18%) than among worshipers age 45 and older (9%). This difference suggests a trend likely to grow in the future—worshipers who participate in but do not join America's congregations.

Catholic worshipers reported slightly less conflict at this level than did Protestants or other faith groups. Only a few worshipers (8%) mentioned major conflict. An even smaller number (4%) said that the conflict resulted in leaders or people leaving the congregation.

Growing Congregations and Types of New People

Congregations with growing worship attendance fuel that growth in several ways. New people (the 33% of all worshipers who have been attending their current congregation for five years or less) come from four different faith backgrounds: *First timers* (8% of all new people) are worshipers who have never regularly attended anywhere. *Returnees* (17% of worshipers attending five years or less) are those who at some point in their life participated in a community of faith and are now returning to worship services. For many returnees, this faith involvement took place when they were children and their parents took them to worship, Sunday or Sabbath school, or other religious activities. A period of absence from active participation is not unusual among worshipers, and this period of inactivity most often occurs during the twenties, with a return to religious activities prompted by marriage or the birth of children.[4]

Most of the growth in congregations comes from the other two types of new people— *switchers* and *transfers*. Switchers, who make up 22% of all new people, move or change from one type of faith community to another. Switching may be prompted by marriage to someone of a different faith background, moving to a new community, or changing values and preferences. Switching has become more common in the United States, with larger numbers of people engaging in "serial switching"— participation in three or more different faith communities during adulthood.

Switching among Protestant groups is more common than moving across the Protestant/Catholic divide or the Christian/non-Christian one. Only 5% of worshipers in Catholic parishes are switchers compared to almost eight times that number (38%)

4. Thomas Rotolo, "A Time to Join, A Time to Quit: The Influence of Life Cycle Transitions on Voluntary Association Membership," *Social Forces* 78, no. 3 (2000): 1133–61.

among worshipers in Protestant churches and congregations of other faith traditions. Non-Catholic worshipers are also more likely to be returnees (22%) than Catholic worshipers (11%).

Transfers—religious participants who move their membership or participation from one congregation to another congregation of the same denomination or faith tradition—have also grown in number. Currently, transfers constitute 54% of new people in U.S. congregations. Greater social and geographic mobility means far fewer Americans stay in one place for a lifetime anymore. As they change jobs and schools, and leave forwarding addresses, many search for a place of worship that is identical to the religious brand they left behind. While some people arrive in a new community and never find another worship site that meets their needs, or are too absorbed with new activities to search out a new worshiping community, many readily pick up their involvement in a congregation of the same denomination or faith tradition. That more than half of all new worshipers are transfers from other congregations indicates that many congregations are circulating regular attendees rather than enlarging the pool of people involved in communities of faith.

The gap between the faith background of new people worshiping in Catholic parishes and those in other congregations appears again when considering transfers. Three out of four new people in Catholic parishes have transferred from other Catholic parishes. Only three in ten (31%) of other worshipers (Protestants and those from other faith traditions) have transferred from a congregation of the same denomination or faith group. (See Figure 5.5.)

What Is There to Do Here?

What do congregations offer participants in addition to opportunities to worship? Many provide religious education, the chance to share with others in a small group, and the possibility of joining a prayer group.

Religious education. Almost all congregations offer a variety of religious education opportunities to worshipers. Most (95%) hold religious education classes, church

TYPES OF NEW PEOPLE*

	All Worshipers	Catholic Worshipers	Protestant and Other Worshipers
First-timers	8%	7%	9%
Returnees	17%	11%	22%
Switchers	22%	5%	38%
Transfers	54%	77%	31%

*New people are those attending the congregation for five years or less.

Figure 5.5

school, or Sabbath school for children. In the average congregation, about 15 children under the age of 12 take part in these classes. Almost 90% also offer similar classes for youth and for adults. About eight youths between 12 and 18 years of age and 20 adults over the age of 18 participate in religious education in the average congregation. (See Figure 5.6.)

Children and youth programs. Most worshipers with children living at home (62%) are satisfied with the activities and programs offered for children and youth (less than 19 years of age) at their congregation. But one-third report mixed feelings or are unsure.

Small groups. A majority of congregations (83%) offer small groups for sharing and spiritual growth, and half of those that do describe their small groups as an important part of their strategy to involve people in the congregation. (See Figure 5.7.)

Group prayer life. Prayer groups meet in most congregations (80%). They include a wide variety of types of groups, convened for many different purposes. (See Figure 5.8.)

RELIGIOUS EDUCATION PROGRAMS

Religious education for . . .

		Average Number of Participants
Children younger than 12 years	95%	15
Youth, ages 12 to 18 years	87%	8
Adults	89%	20

Figure 5.6

SMALL GROUPS OR CELLS

Important part of congregation's strategy . . .

To involve people	44%
To foster spiritual development and discipleship	42%
To involve people in community service or ministry	22%

Figure 5.7

What Matters?

The majority of worshipers are attending services but participating in little or nothing else in their congregation. The thin layer of engagement in the congregation's total offerings means that many worshipers miss out on a variety of opportunities available to them. The majority are not taking part in any small-group activity, serving as leaders, or getting involved in making congregational decisions. The majority are not major financial stakeholders, given their low levels of regular giving. Despite these behavioral patterns among worshipers, they *feel* connected to their parish or congregation. The

TYPES OF PRAYER GROUPS

Prayer groups that meet infrequently or only at certain times of the year......... 15%

Regular prayer groups that are part of a small-group or cell program
    or are attached to specific classes, groups, or ministries........................... 33%

Other types of prayer groups 50%

No organized prayer groups.. 20%

Figure 5.8

average worshiper makes close friends in his or her community of faith and has a strong sense of belonging

What is the faith background of new people in the average congregation? The largest group among those attending for five years or less in Catholic parishes is transfers—those moving their membership or involvement from one Catholic parish to another. In the average Protestant congregation the largest numbers are switchers—those moving their involvement to a congregation in a different denomination than the one they previously attended. The number of new people who are becoming involved in a faith community for the first time is quite small. Congregations are doing a far better job of attracting worshipers who have a history of parish or congregational association.

CHAPTER 6

OUTSIDE CONNECTIONS

Every species depends on its habitat to survive. Congregations likewise exist in time and space occupying a specific habitat. This chapter deals with the relationships that worshipers have with their habitat—the local community of the congregation or parish. How do they make outside connections? Located in communities that are growing or declining, they welcome new people or say good-bye more times than they'd like. Some parishes are struggling to relate to large numbers of new people who speak a variety of languages. In some places, wheelchair-accessible ramps replace basketball hoops as the neighborhood changes from one teeming with young families to one full of empty-nest older couples. Congregations have a stake in their habitat indicated by their strong sense of place, a feeling of belonging to a particular piece of geography—their corner of the neighborhood, city, town, or county. How are congregations fed by their communities? Or more important, how do congregations and parishes feed, both spiritually and materially, their communities?

Some faith traditions make a clear distinction between two possible ways to relate to their context. One type of relating to the congregation's context is evangelism or efforts to bring new people into the faith community. Individual members and regular worshipers act to include outsiders in their faith community by inviting others and sharing their faith. A second avenue for relating to the community is through social service or advocacy efforts. Some see this second approach as another strategy for bringing new people into the congregation rather than a distinct ministry activity that may or may not result in new members. Both categories of relating to the community can be the result of individual efforts by worshipers or a collective strategy carried out by the congregation itself. Evangelism, or reaching out to nonmembers, is described below. Community service and advocacy efforts are described in the section that follows.

Reaching Out to Nonmembers

Inviting behavior. Less than half of worshipers (43%) invited someone—a friend or relative who is not currently attending a church, synagogue, or temple—to a worship service at their congregation in the past year. About as many (41%) say they are prepared to do so, but haven't in the past year. Worshipers in Catholic parishes are less likely to have issued such an invitation than are worshipers in other types of congregations. (See Figure 6.1.)

Talking the walk. Three out of four worshipers (74%) say they find it easy to talk about their faith, and some of these (16% overall) seek opportunities to do so. Others (11%) do not talk about their faith because they believe their life and actions are sufficient. (See Figure 6.2.)

Congregational efforts. In addition to the efforts of individual worshipers to invite others, most congregations and parishes collectively act to let others know of their services and programs (such as providing a Web site for the congregation). From a list of 15 such outreach activities (see Figure 6.3), congregations most often report encouraging their current worshipers to invite someone new to the congregation. Many send letters or other information to people who have already visited the congregation or parish. Other common strategies by congregations include mailing newsletters or flyers; hosting

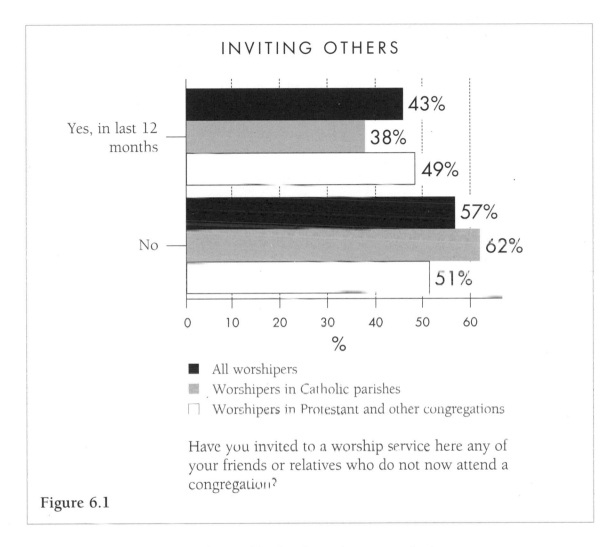

INVITING OTHERS

Yes, in last 12 months
- 43%
- 38%
- 49%

No
- 57%
- 62%
- 51%

- ■ All worshipers
- ▨ Worshipers in Catholic parishes
- ☐ Worshipers in Protestant and other congregations

Have you invited to a worship service here any of your friends or relatives who do not now attend a congregation?

Figure 6.1

an activity to meet people in the neighborhood; or placing a paid ad in a newspaper or magazine. On average, congregations report using seven of these techniques.

Congregations also use other methods to include more people in their worship services, denomination, or faith tradition. Some have reorganized or started a new worship service for a distinct age, racial or ethnic, socioeconomic, or interest group (7%).

TALKING ABOUT FAITH

Which of the following best describes your readiness to talk to others about your faith?

I do not have faith, so the question is not applicable.. 1%

I do not talk about my faith; my life and actions are sufficient........................ 11%

I find it hard to talk about my faith in ordinary language............................... 13%

I mostly feel at ease talking about my faith and do so if it comes up............... 58%

I feel at ease talking about my faith and seek opportunities to do so............... 16%

Figure 6.2

And others (5%) have reorganized or started a new worship service for people who do not normally attend (often called "seeker services"). A few (6%) have been involved in planting or growing a new congregation in the previous five years.

How are new members integrated? Once a worshiper has joined, most congregations use planned procedures to ensure the new person becomes involved. Two out of three congregations follow up by inviting new members to take on a task within the congregation. Half of congregations invite newcomers to join a small group of some kind. Congregations may also offer a group or course for new members (36%).

Serving the Community

On my own—doing community service or advocacy. Many pastors describe their congregation as a group of worshipers who are highly involved in community service or advocacy work *not* connected to the local congregation. They believe that being involved in congregational activities leads people of faith to engage in social service and social justice work. Is this the case? Yes. In fact, *more* worshipers are active in community ser-

CONGREGATIONAL OUTREACH ACTIVITIES

Encouraged people already in the congregation to invite a new person 87%

Established or maintained a Web site for the congregation 77%

Sent a letter or material to people who visited your congregation 76%

Mailed or distributed newsletters, letters, or flyers 70%

Had an activity (e.g., fair, chili supper) to meet people in the neighborhood 58%

Placed a paid ad in a newspaper or magazine 51%

Sponsored or participated in a worship service or other
   public event intended to bring people into your congregation 46%

Had someone from the congregation telephone people who
   visited your congregation 45%

Placed a paid ad in the phone book or yellow pages 36%

Had someone from the congregation go to the home of people who
   visited your congregation 32%

Tried to identify and contact people who recently moved into the area 30%

Had a special committee to work on recruiting new members 30%

Sent an e-mail to people who visited the congregation 29%

Advertised on radio or TV 15%

Conducted or used a survey of the community 7%

Figure 6.3

vice or advocacy work in the community apart from their congregation (34%) than are involved in the congregation's service and advocacy activities (18%). If they are involved in such work outside their congregation, they are five times more likely to be active in social service or charity groups (32%) than in advocacy, justice, or lobbying groups (6%). (See Figure 6.4.)

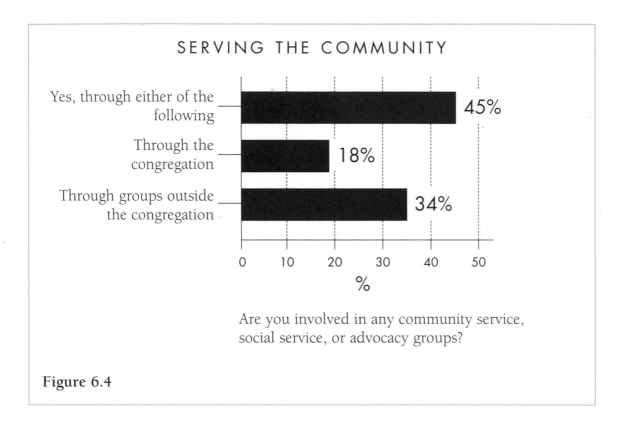

SERVING THE COMMUNITY

Yes, through either of the following — 45%

Through the congregation — 18%

Through groups outside the congregation — 34%

0   10   20   30   40   50

%

Are you involved in any community service, social service, or advocacy groups?

Figure 6.4

Many congregations also send groups or individual members to areas where people need assistance (e.g., places affected by Hurricane Katrina). Four in ten congregations sent individuals to some part of the United States for such aid in the previous year, and 29% sent people or groups to another country to lend volunteer assistance. Overall 6% of worshipers went on a mission or service trip in the prior year. (See Figure 6.5.)

Individual charity begins at home. Worshipers are often thought of as "good neighbors"—always giving and helpful to others. In fact, they are. In the 12 months before the survey, many prepared or gave food to someone outside their family or congregation (50%), loaned money to someone outside the family (28%), helped someone find a job (23%), or cared for someone outside their family who was very sick (22%). Most worshipers (73%) gave money to a charitable organization (other than the congregation) in the past year. (See Figure 6.6.)

Acts of advocacy and politics. Worshipers are more likely to vote than the average American. Eight in ten worshipers (83%) say they voted in the last presidential election.[1] Only about 62% of eligible Americans voted for president in 2008.[2] In addition,

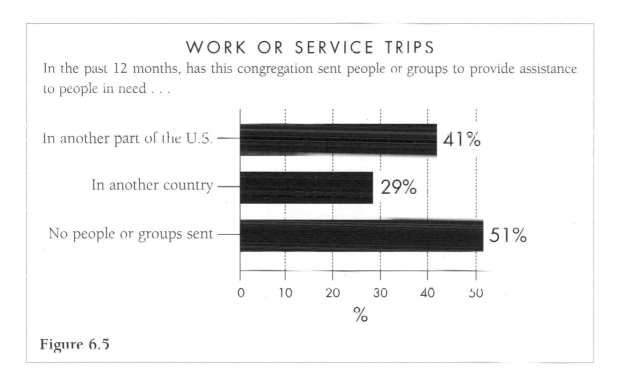

WORK OR SERVICE TRIPS

In the past 12 months, has this congregation sent people or groups to provide assistance to people in need . . .

In another part of the U.S. — 41%

In another country — 29%

No people or groups sent — 51%

%

Figure 6.5

1. Some participating congregations completed the worship surveys prior to the November 4, 2008, election. Additional congregations took part by completing the worship surveys in the spring of 2009.

2. *Civic Engagement: Survey of Voters and Nonvoters* (Evanston, IL: Medill School of Journalism, Northwestern University, March 2001). Michael McDonald, "United States Election Project" (George Mason University, Fairfax, VA), http://elections.gmu.edu/preliminary_vote_2008.html; updated January 11, 2009; retrieved on January 28, 2009. Eligible voters are U.S. citizens 18 and older who are not felons. The 62% statistic is based on these eligible voters, not on registered voters or the entire U.S. population.

worshipers are involved in the political arena in other ways: In the previous year, one in five (20%) worked with others to try to solve a community problem and 18% contacted an elected official about a public issue.[3] (See Figure 6.7.)

During religious services, worshipers in 91% of congregations are told about volunteer opportunities to assist others in the community. Fewer congregations inform worshipers about opportunities for political activity (25%) or share information about voter registration (38%).

Services offered through the congregation. We asked each congregation which of 25 services they have provided for people in the community or for their members in the past year (see Figure 6.8). The average congregation reported involvement in six areas. Only two were cited by a large majority of congregations—emergency relief and counseling or support groups.

3. The General Social Survey (GSS), National Opinion Research Center at the University of Chicago, asked about both of these topics in a slightly different manner. GSS respondents were asked if they had *ever* worked with others to try to solve a community problem, and 33% said yes. Among worshipers, 21% had done so *in the previous year*. GSS respondents were also asked if they had contacted or attempted to contact a politician or a civil servant to express their views in the past year (2006), and 22% said yes. Among worshipers, 19% had contacted an elected official *in the previous year*. The somewhat lower participation rates for worshipers are not surprising given that they were focusing on the previous year rather than a lifetime of possible political involvement.

ACTS OF CHARITY

In the past 12 months, have you done any of the following? (Mark *all* that apply.)

Donated money to a charitable organization (other than this congregation).... 73%
Donated or prepared food for someone outside your family or congregation.. 50%
Loaned money to someone outside your family 28%
Helped someone outside your family find a job 23%
Cared for someone outside your family who was very sick 22%
Went on a mission or service trip 6%

Figure 6.6

ACTS OF ADVOCACY AND POLITICS

In the past 12 months, have you done any of the following? (Mark *all* that apply.)

Will vote or did vote in the 2008 presidential election* 83%
Worked with others to try to solve a community problem............................. 20%
Contacted an elected official about a public issue 18%
Contributed money to a political party or candidate 16%

*Some participating congregations completed the worship surveys before the November 2008 election. Calculated for those 18 and older.

Figure 6.7

TYPES OF COMMUNITY SERVICE

Emergency relief or material assistance (food, clothes for the needy) 87%

Counseling or support groups (marriage or bereavement counseling) 59%

Other social, recreational, or leisure activities 52%

Transportation to bring people to worship services.. 51%

Other programs for children and youth (scouting, sports) 49%

Art, music, or cultural activities or programs 44%

Health-related programs and activities (blood drives, screenings) 37%

Other senior-citizen programs or assistance (Meals on Wheels, transportation)..... 37%

Other community service or social action activities not mentioned here 30%

Hobby or craft groups... 29%

Sporting activities or teams (intramural teams) 22%

Political or social justice activities (civil rights, human rights)............................ 22%

Voter registration or voter education... 20%

Substance abuse or 12-step recovery programs 20%

Prison or jail ministry... 19%

Programs or activities for college students... 18%

Housing for other groups (crisis, youth shelters, homeless, students) 18%

Care for persons with disabilities (skills training, respite care, home care)........... 16%

Community-organizing or neighborhood-action groups 14%

Immigrant support activities (refugee support, interpreting)............................. 12%

Financial literacy programs or help with budgeting or debt management 12%

Animal welfare or environmental activities... 11%

Programs or services for persons with HIV or AIDS.................................... 5%

Activities for unemployed people (job-seeking preparation, skills training) 3%

Housing for senior citizens (nursing homes, assisted living) 3%

Figure 6.8

What Matters?

Congregations and parishes connect with their communities by welcoming new people and serving society's needs. Most congregations rely on informal, person-to-person contact to alert people in the community that they are welcome at worship services. Many also use electronic and print media (e.g., Web site, newspaper ads) to convey their welcoming message. Almost four out of five have established a presence on the Internet as a way to connect to people in their community.

An individual approach surfaces again when characterizing the ways congregations relate to community needs. Individual worshipers carry out many such efforts (e.g., voting, contacting elected officials, donating to charitable organizations). Acting collectively, congregations are most likely to help those in need through providing emergency relief in the form of food or clothes. Counseling or support groups are also offered by a majority of congregations. While these types of efforts are enormously important in any community, they tend not to address the ongoing systemic problems that may have given rise to individual and family distress. For example, job training, community organizing, and housing programs aimed at community social change are less likely to be undertaken by congregations.

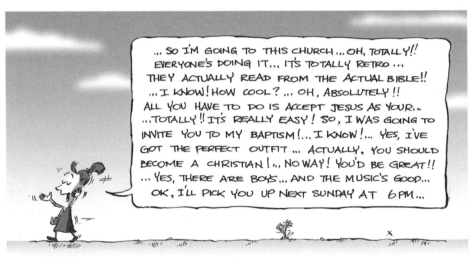

CHAPTER 7

Types of Worshipers

A field guide promises a comprehensive profile of all the specific subspecies in a general category. For example, did you know there are fifty-two different breeds of cows? Subspecies are simply subcategories or subdivisions of a general category. In this chapter, the field guide describes some of the many types of worshipers—frequent attendees and new people, for example—and their unique field marks. The worshiper subspecies are arranged in order from the most common (the frequent worshiper who attends services every week) to the more rare or exotic (someone visiting a congregation for the first time).

The 76%: Weekly Worshipers

The most common worshiper is someone who reports attending every week.[1] Surprisingly, this group makes up 76% of all worshipers. Are they different in any way from the less frequent worshiper—the 24% who attend services occasionally?

---

1. Because the survey was given in worship, more frequent attendees are more likely to have been present on the day it was given. For example, someone who attends worship services every week is sure to have been there no matter which week the survey was given. Someone who attends only once a month would be far less likely to have been in worship on that day.

Long-term attendance. Long-term commitment to the congregation yields higher rates of worship attendance. Weekly worshipers are more likely to be found among those who have been attending the congregation for more than 20 years. Nine out of ten of those long-term attendees, but only 67% of those attending two years or less, attend weekly.

Denomination or faith group. Worshipers in Catholic parishes are just as likely to be frequent attendees as worshipers from other faith groups.

Involvement in other activities. Those who attend worship week after week are twice as likely as occasional worshipers to be involved in congregational small groups (such as church or Sabbath school; prayer, discussion, or Bible study groups; or social or fellowship groups) and other congregational activities (such as evangelism or community service). They are also almost three times more likely to hold a leadership position in the parish or congregation.

Big givers. Worshipers who attend weekly are three times as likely as other worshipers to give 10% or more of their income to the congregation (21% compared to just 6%). Weekly worshipers are twice as likely to give 5% or more of their income (32% compared to 15%). Clearly, regular attendance fosters greater financial support for the congregation. A large percentage of occasional attendees (37%) report they give a small amount whenever they are in services.

Gender. While more women sit in the pews, there is barely a difference in how frequently men and women attend services. Women are only slightly more likely to attend worship on a weekly basis than men. Sixty-two percent of all frequent worshipers are women; 59% of less frequent worshipers are women.

Age. People 65 years of age and older attend services more frequently than the average worshiper. Younger adults under 44 years of age attend religious services less frequently than worshipers in other age groups.

Work. Frequent worshipers are more likely to be retired than those who attend less often. Occasional worshipers are more likely to report full- or part-time employment.

Education and income. Surprisingly, looking at education *and* household income helps us identify frequent worshipers. Weekly worshipers are less educated than those who attend occasionally. Additionally, weekly attendees have lower household incomes than worshipers who do not attend on a weekly basis.

Race, ethnicity, and nationality. Whites are slightly more likely to be weekly attendees than black or Hispanic attendees. There are no differences in attendance for Asian, Native American, or other racial or ethnic worshipers when compared to white worshipers. Weekly worshipers are slightly more likely to have been born in the United States. Current residents born outside the United States—particularly in non-English-speaking countries—are less frequent in their attendance than other worshipers.

Marital status and children. Married worshipers are slightly more likely to go to religious services on a weekly basis. Those who have never been married are less frequent in their worship attendance. Widowed people are also overrepresented among the weekly worshipers, being almost twice as likely to be present as other types of singles. People with children residing at home are less frequent in their attendance than those with no children at home.

Travel time. It's not living closer that gets weekly worshipers there more often. Frequent attendees spend the same amount of time traveling to worship as those who come less often. (See Figure 7.1.)

THE 76%—WEEKLY WORSHIPERS: A PROFILE

Women	62%
65 years of age or older	34%
Retired	32%
College or more advanced degree	43%
Married	66%
No children residing at home	59%
Attending more than 20 years	33%
Involved in a small group	60%
Hold a leadership role	47%
Give 10% or more	21%

Figure 7.1

The 33%: New People

As mentioned in chapter 5, worshipers can be divided into three approximately equal-sized groups. About one in three (33%) are new people, that is, worshipers attending services at their current congregation five years or less. Another third (34%) have been attending services there between 6 and 20 years. And a final third (29%) have been attending more than 20 years. (About 4% are visitors from another congregation or people who don't regularly attend anywhere else.) The proportion of new people attending worship services suggests a fairly high turnover rate in the average faith community. What are the field marks of worshipers who have been attending for five years or less?

Denomination or faith group. The pool of new worshipers is slightly larger in Protestant churches and congregations of other faith groups than in Catholic parishes.

Low levels of involvement. Fewer new people are involved in small groups of any type (36% of new people compared to 45% for all worshipers). The biggest gap in their small-group involvement compared to other worshipers is in their participation in congregational social or fellowship groups (20% participate compared to 28% for all worshipers). Even more significant is their lower rate of holding leadership roles in the congregation. These findings suggest that the entrance ramps to congregational involvement at a leadership level are long and narrow.

The pattern of less involvement in congregational activities appears in a third way.

New people are less likely to take part in activities of the congregation or parish that involve outreach, evangelism, community service, or advocacy.

Giving. The giving patterns of new people reflect their lower levels of involvement. New people are somewhat less likely than long-term participants to give 10% or more of their income to the congregation. Further, new worshipers report lower levels of regular giving (between 5% and 9%) when compared to long-term worshipers. They are more likely to give just small amounts of money whenever they attend services.

Age. New people are younger than the average worshiper by nine years. The largest percentage of new worshipers (37%) are in the 25-to-44-year-old age group. Less than one-quarter of all worshipers fall in the same age bracket.

Work. Working full- or part-time is more common among the newer worshipers. In fact, almost three-quarters of new people are employed. This finding is clearly related to the lower average age of these worshipers.

Education. As educated as the average worshiper, many new people hold college degrees or more advanced degrees (48%), and a large group have attained a high school diploma or more education (91%).

Race, ethnicity, and nationality. Compared to long-term worshipers, people new in their congregations are less likely to be white and less likely to have been born in the United States. Fewer new people are native English speakers.

Marital status. New people are less likely than long-term participants to be in their first marriage. They are more likely than longtime worshipers to have never married or to be remarried after divorce. Again, these patterns are probably associated with the average age of new worshipers.

Nondistinguishing field marks. While new people look different from long-term worshipers in some ways, in other ways they are quite similar. New people are similar to typical worshipers in terms of gender and income (about one-third in each group earn $75,000 or more). (See Figure 7.2.)

The 24%: Younger Worshipers

Many believe that younger people are largely missing from the pews in America's congregations. But that's not true. They certainly aren't in the majority, but they are in worship. How do younger worshipers—the 24% who are between the ages of 25 and 44—differ from older worshipers? Other than being younger, what sets them apart?

Involvement. For the most part, the involvement of younger worshipers in their congregations does not reach the level of older worshipers. Younger worshipers attend worship services less often, make smaller financial contributions, are less likely to be

---

THE 33%—NEW PEOPLE: A PROFILE*

Women	60%
25 to 44 years of age	37%
Employed full- or part-time	64%
College or more advanced degree	48%
Married	62%
No children residing at home	51%
Involved in a small group	36%
Hold a leadership role	28%
Give 10% or more	16%

*New people are those attending for five years or less.

Figure 7.2

---

members (or to be in the process of becoming members) of the congregation, and are less likely to participate in prayer or Bible study groups or serve in a leadership role. But there is some good news! Compared to older worshipers, younger people participate more in church school or other religious education groups. They also sing in the choir and help lead church school classes at about the same rate as other worshipers.

Serving others. Younger worshipers are less likely than older worshipers to be involved in the congregation's evangelism or social service activities. However, assisting on a personal level, they are more likely to have loaned someone money or helped someone find a job.

Worship experiences and preferences. Younger worshipers (ages 25–44) experience God's presence during worship services about as often as older worshipers. While a majority of older worshipers (63%) prefer traditional music in worship, more younger worshipers prefer praise music, contemporary hymns, and other contemporary music.

Private devotions. Unlike older worshipers, six in ten people ages 25–44 (61%) spend time in private devotional activities more than once a week. This group does not come close to the frequency of Bible reading and private prayer of older worshipers, 71% of whom engage in private devotional activities more than once a week.

Employment and income. Four in five worshipers ages 25–44 work either full- or part-time (83%). In contrast, fewer worshipers 45 and older are employed (52%). Household income follows these differences. Only 14% of worshipers between the ages of 25 and 44 earn less than $25,000 annually, and 19% of those who are older report similar incomes.

Education. Worshipers between 25 and 44 years of age are more educated than older worshipers. Somewhat more than half of these younger worshipers report obtaining a college degree or more advanced degrees.

More diversity. Compared to older worshipers, younger worshipers are less likely to be white, more likely to have been born outside the United States, and more likely to have spoken a language other than English when they were five years old. Despite this increase in diversity, the majority of younger worshipers are white, born in the United States, and native English speakers.

Marital status and children. Most younger worshipers are married. Seven in ten worshipers ages 25 to 44 live in households that include children. In contrast, only 30% of worshipers age 45 or older live with children. (See Figure 7.3.)

The 2%: First-Time Worship Visitors

Every congregation invites and welcomes visitors to its services. Yet across worship services in more than 5,000 American congregations, only 2% of those attending were present in that congregation for the first time. Who are these rare worshipers? What are their field marks?

Denomination or faith group. Catholic parishes were more likely to have first-time visitors attending their Masses than Protestant churches or other congregations had attending their worship services.

History of worship attendance. The majority of first-time visitors (67%) reported they had been participating in another congregation before coming to worship in one

---

THE 24%—YOUNGER WORSHIPERS: A PROFILE*

Women.. 61%
Employed full- or part-time 83%
College or more advanced degree 56%
Married... 73%
Children residing at home 73%
Involved in a small group 41%
Hold a leadership role...32%
Give 10% or more 15%

*Younger worshipers are those between ages 25 and 44.

Figure 7.3

---

of the study's congregations. But 14% said they had never regularly attended anywhere before visiting the congregation. Another 16% said that prior to visiting this congregation they had not been attending anywhere for several years.

Gender. More first-time worship visitors are women than men (61% compared to 39%), a gender ratio almost identical to all worshipers.

Age. The largest group of first-time worship visitors (34%) consists of people between the ages of 25 and 44. The average age of these rare worshipers is 43, fully 11 years younger than the average worshiper.

Work. Visitors look quite similar to all worshipers in terms of their employment profile. Most (58%) are working full- or part-time. However, more students and fewer retired people are found among the first-time visitors than in the general worshiper population.

Marital status. While only one-third of all worshipers are not married, a larger portion (46%) of all first-time worship visitors are not married. One in four (26%) of these visitors have never been married; 10% are divorced or separated; 5% are living in a committed relationship but are not married; and 5% are widowed. (See Figure 7.4.)

What Matters?

Why identify types of worshipers? The answer goes to the heart of the congregation's purpose: What are we trying to do here? What is God calling us to do and be as a congregation? People sitting in the pews may look like average Americans to the uninformed observer. However, chapter 2 illustrates that worshipers are far from typical Americans, and this chapter shows that worshipers differ from one another in important ways. Often, we make easy assumptions about why people come, what types of people are going to be most committed, and what must be done to "fix" what we think doesn't work. Programs, strategies, planning, and all sorts of efforts can be made that yield little in terms of furthering the congregation's mission.

Like bird-watching, not too much gear is needed to spot types of worshipers. Look for clues in terms of the factors discussed in this chapter and ask: What kind of worshipers are they? Knowing "who comes to worship services" is the first step in thinking about

THE 2%—FIRST-TIME VISITORS: A PROFILE

Women	61%
25 to 44 years of age	34%
Employed full- or part-time	58%
Married	54%
Attending elsewhere recently	67%
Returning after long-term absence	16%
Never regularly attended anywhere	14%

Figure 7.4

"why people come." To better understand "why they come," review the field marks of weekly worshipers, new people, younger worshipers, and first-time visitors. Who are congregations currently attracting and welcoming to their worship services and congregational activities? Why is this the case?

The field marks of worshipers laid out in this chapter are meant to assist leaders in seeing their congregation in bold relief. What are the characteristics that make your congregation stand out? Use these as clues as you seek to answer the most important question: "What are we trying to accomplish here?"

CHAPTER 8

LEADERSHIP

Who provides the key leadership for congregations? Congregations are voluntary organizations usually guided by full- or part-time ministerial staff. The full leadership team typically includes laypeople—those without seminary degrees or special ordination status—and clergy, such as pastors, priests, rabbis, or imams. In this chapter, we first describe the latter group, the senior or solo pastors in congregations who are ordained or seeking ordination.[1] Typically, their denomination or faith group ordains them to carry out official duties for the congregation.[2] The history of American clergy leadership is one of dramatic change, especially in the demographic profile of those assuming this vital role in religious life. The second part of this chapter focuses on worshipers' perceptions of their pastor, priest, or rabbi and his or her leadership style.

1. The first section of this chapter focuses on findings from a survey completed by one key leader in each congregation participating in the U.S. Congregational Life Survey. The leader profile is drawn from the national random sample of congregations, whether their worshipers completed surveys or not. The leader sample data were weighted to adjust for congregational size. Because larger congregations were more likely to be nominated, larger congregations have a higher probability of appearing in the sample. Weighting the sample by size provides results that accurately reflect the size distribution of congregations in the United States. The profile excludes associate pastors and pastoral leaders who are neither ordained nor seeking ordination. Fewer than 2% of the senior and solo pastors were not ordained or seeking ordination, and they are excluded from this analysis.

2. The view of pastoral leadership as an office sets the individual apart from the congregation. Ordination legitimizes the pastor's special role in administering sacraments, preaching, teaching, and general administrative responsibility for the congregation. See Jackson Carroll, *God's Potters* (Grand Rapids: Wm. B. Eerdmans Publishing Co., 2006), for a full discussion of the contrasting views of pastoral leadership as office, profession, and calling.

How to Identify a Clergy Leader

Gender. Male clergy still outnumber women in almost every Christian faith tradition.[3] Only men can be ordained as Catholic priests, and male clergy take the lead in most conservative Protestant congregations as well. However, women have established a place in ministry in many mainline Protestant groups. Mainline Protestant congregations welcome a substantial number of female clergy—one in four of these churches are served by a woman in the senior or solo pastor position.[4] (See Figure 8.1.)

   Age. The average age of clergy is 56—about the same as other professionals with similar education (master's, doctorate, or other postgraduate degree).[5] Average clergy ages differ by denominational tradition, with Catholic priests being the oldest group of clergy.

GENDER OF CLERGY BY DENOMINATIONAL TRADITION

	Catholic	Mainline Protestant	Conservative Protestant
Male	100%	72%	100%
Female	0%	28%	0%

Figure 8.1

---

3. Edward Lehman, *Women's Path into Ministry: Six Major Studies* (Durham, NC: Pulpit and Pew Research Reports, Duke Divinity School, 2002), www.pulpitandpew.duke.edu.

4. Because clergywomen are more likely to hold associate or assistant positions in congregations and these positions are not included here, the percentages in Figure 8.1 do not reflect the full range of female leadership in congregational life.

5. For Catholic priests, the average age in 2001 was 56 (now 61 in our sample); for mainline Protestant clergy, it was 51 (now 55 in our sample); and for conservative Protestant clergy, it was 50 (now 55 in our sample). See Carroll, *God's Potters,* 71–72.

Overall, clergy serving in congregations are older than in the past. In 1968, for example, 56% of mainline clergy and 54% of conservative Protestant clergy were less than 45 years of age.[6] This "graying" of the American clergy stems from several factors. Recently fewer young people have been entering seminary or ministry immediately following their college graduation. The average age of entering theological students rose by more than ten years between 1962 and 2005. Previous research also indicates that older students show more interest in serving as local church pastors.[7] Plus more clergy are "second career"—entering ministry after a career in another field or retirement. Some second-career clergy are women whose family responsibilities received priority in earlier decades. (See Figure 8.2.)

Second-career clergy. More than half (59%) of ordained clergy worked full-time

AGE OF CLERGY BY DENOMINATIONAL TRADITION

	Catholic	Mainline Protestant	Conservative Protestant	Total
Under 45	9%	16%	17%	16%
45–50	12%	15%	24%	17%
51–60	27%	44%	34%	40%
Over 60	51%	25%	26%	27%
Median Age	61	55	55	56

Figure 8.2

6. Carroll, *God's Potters*, 72 (original data from Edgar Mills).
7. Barbara Wheeler, Sharon Miller, and Daniel Aleshire, "How Are We Doing? The Effectiveness of Theological Schools as Measured by the Vocations and Views of Graduates," *Auburn Studies*, no. 13 (December 2007); Barbara Wheeler, "Is There a Problem? Theological Students and Religious Leadership for the Future," *Auburn Studies*, no. 8 (2001).

at one or more occupations before entering the ministry. One way to track this second-career trend is to compare the average age at ordination among clergy who have been in ministry for different lengths of time. This comparison shows that those who entered the ministry more recently (serving less than 10 years) were substantially older when they were ordained than long-term clergy (those serving for more than 10 years) were at their ordination. For example, the age of first-decade clergy at the time of their ordination varies from an average of 48 years for Catholic priests, to 43 years for mainline Protestant clergy, and 38 years for conservative Protestant clergy. In contrast, clergy in their fourth decade of ministry—regardless of faith group—were ordained (on average) at about age 26. (See Figure 8.3.)

AGE OF CLERGY AT ORDINATION BY YEARS IN MINISTRY AND DENOMINATIONAL TRADITION*

Years in Ministry	Less than 10	10–20	21–30	31-plus
Catholic	48	31	31	27
Mainline Protestant	43	37	29	26
Conservative Protestant	38	34	30	26
All Denominations	43	36	29	26

*Median age reported

Figure 8.3

AVERAGE SALARY OF SENIOR OR SOLO PASTORS BY CONGREGATIONAL SIZE*

	Catholic	Mainline Protestant	Conservative Protestant
Size of congregation			
Small (fewer than 100 in worship)	$30,660	$45,900	$38,632
Medium (100–350 in worship)	$36,295	$60,045	$51,761
Large (more than 350 in worship)	$34,866	$87,082	$78,886
All Sizes	$32,300	$52,300	$46,000

*Salary includes housing compensation; medians reported

Figure 8.4

Compensation. The salary structure for Catholic priests is basically a flat one—compensation does not vary much by the size of the parish. However, clergy salaries among Protestant groups are closely tied to the size of the congregation. On average, mainline Protestant clergy earn more than their conservative Protestant colleagues. (See Figure 8.4.)

With some assistance. Three out of four congregations employ just one full-time, ordained clergy leader. Yet additional pastoral leadership is provided by paid nonordained ministerial staff in many congregations. Larger congregations more often benefit from multiple staff. For example, congregations with more than 350 in worship average almost five full-time, paid staff, including ordained clergy, lay ministers, and other pastoral leaders. (See Figure 8.5.)

AVERAGE SIZE OF PAID STAFF (ORDAINED CLERGY AND PASTORAL LEADERS) BY CONGREGATIONAL SIZE*

Number of Employees: Full-time equivalent ordained professionals and pastoral leaders

Fewer than 100 in worship	1.0
100–350 in worship	1.5
More than 350 in worship	4.5

*Median number of paid staff reported

Figure 8.5

How Worshipers Describe Their Leader

What do people in the pew have to say about their key leader? We asked worshipers to describe their leader's style of working with people and how he or she gets people involved. Worshipers and their leaders were also asked whether they believe there is a good match between the congregation and the minister, pastor, or priest.

Leadership style of pastor. Half of attendees (50%) portray the leadership style of the minister, pastor, or priest as one that inspires people to take action. Others (16%) describe their leader's style as one "that tends to take charge." A reactive style, "leadership that acts on goals that people here have been involved in setting," is also reported by 16% of worshipers. Even fewer (2%) say "the people start most things" in their congregation. (See Figure 8.6.)

Ministers take into account worshipers' ideas. In general worshipers say their minister, pastor, or priest takes into account the ideas of those who worship in the congregation to "a great extent" (44%) or to "some extent" (28%). Some "don't know" (22%) whether the minister is open to others' ideas. Only 1% describe their leader as someone who doesn't take into account the ideas of worshipers.

Another good sign. The majority (78%) report their congregation's leaders have encouraged them to find and use their gifts and skills in the congregation or parish. But one in five worshipers (21%) say this encouragement has not happened at all or "don't know" if it has.

Being a team. Do worshipers feel allied with the key leader in the congregation? About half of worshipers strongly agree with the statement "In general, there is a good match between our congregation and our minister, pastor, or priest," and another 34% agree. A very small number (only 3%) believe their leader and congregation are not a good match, and the rest are neutral or unsure (12%). Unfortunately, a small number of unhappy people, especially if they hold leadership positions, can disrupt the harmony of congregational or parish life.

> # MYTH TRAP
>
> ## Most pastors work seven days a week.
>
> *Worshipers sometimes assume that is true, and pastors may feel that it is true. But in fact, 88% of pastors regularly take off at least one day each week. Among those who do so, 31% take off Monday and 46% take off Friday. Nonetheless, clergy work, on average, 50 hours per week, so they pack a lot into the remaining six days.*

Conservative Protestant worshipers indicated the strongest sense that the pastor is a good match for the congregation. In Catholic parishes, the smallest proportion of worshipers strongly agree that their priest is a good match for their congregation. (See Figure 8.7.)

The satisfaction with their leader expressed by worshipers varies from one congregation to another. Worshipers in faith groups where congregations are assigned a priest or pastor—for example, Catholic parishes and Methodist churches—were less likely to view their leader as a good match. Worshipers in denominations where congregations are free to choose their own leaders with little or no direction from higher church officials tend to be happier with their choice.[8]

8. These findings are consistent with the 2001 survey results reported by Jackson Carroll in *God's Potters*. See Figure 3.3 (p. 86) in that book for a more detailed breakdown of worshiper satisfaction with the key leader by denomination or faith group.

LEADERSHIP STYLE OF PASTOR

Leadership that tends to take charge 16%

Leadership that inspires people to take action.. 50%

Leadership that acts on goals that people here have been
    involved in setting.. 16%

Leadership where the people start most things.. 2%

There is currently no leader here 1%

Don't know.. 15%

Figure 8.6

WORSHIPERS' PERCEPTION OF LEADERSHIP MATCH

There is a good match between our congregation and our pastor
or pastoral leader.

	Strongly Agree
Catholic..	48%
Mainline Protestant	52%
Conservative Protestant	61%
All Denominations	51%

Figure 8.7

Leaders' views. Key leaders were asked whether they agree with a similar statement: "In general, there is a good match between this congregation and my leadership." Overall, 48% of the leaders strongly agreed. The strength of leaders' agreement was about the same as that of worshipers (worshipers, 51%; leaders, 48%). (See Figure 8.8.)

The gap between worshipers' views and their leader's view was largest in Catholic parishes where priests were much more likely than their worshipers to see a match (a difference of 15 percentage points). In contrast, conservative Protestant pastors were much *less* likely than their worshipers to see a match (a difference of 14 percentage points). Mainline Protestant clergy were also less likely to see a good match than their worshipers, but the gap was less dramatic (a difference of 4 percentage points).

What Matters?

Most worshipers are satisfied with the key leader in their congregation. Worshipers describe their leaders as inspiring others and as taking their ideas into account. Yet

---

LEADERS' PERCEPTION OF CONGREGATIONAL MATCH

There is a good match between this congregation and my leadership.

	Strongly Agree
Catholic	63%
Mainline Protestant	48%
Conservative Protestant	47%
All Denominations	48%

Figure 8.8

American congregations face several leadership challenges—aging clergy, continued resistance to female clergy, and the inability to compensate clergy commensurate with their education and experience.[9] Two factors—congregational size and denomination or faith group—significantly impact clergy compensation. And the congregation's denomination or faith group affords a framework for the degree of satisfaction worshipers experience with their leader.

How will America's congregations face these problems in the years to come? Already some are pursuing alternative staffing models such as lay pastoral leaders and yoked or multipoint parishes. Will these new models sustain worshipers' currently positive opinions of their pastoral leaders? Further, how can congregations and their leaders encourage women and young adults to pursue ministry? We can be reassured in knowing that despite these leadership obstacles, today's congregational leaders find the call to ministry to be fulfilling and satisfying work.

9. Carroll, *God's Potters*, 219–34.

IN THAT MOMENT, REV. WALLACE KNEW THAT HE HAD NAILED THE CHURCH'S NEW VISION STATEMENT.

CHAPTER 9

CONGREGATIONAL IDENTITY AND VISION

This chapter covers the trickiest and yet most crucial part of any guided exploration: Where are we headed? What is our sense of direction? Where do we think we're going? Any guide can be of only limited use if we have little idea about our future destination. What is our goal and in which direction should we take our first step?

Congregations, like people, live in the present. But they have a story about their past that gives meaning to the present. Likewise, they have a mental map about what the future looks like. Is the future more of the same or does it look radically different? Another contribution of this guide is to explore two interrelated themes: identity—who we think we are, and vision—what the depth and breadth of our future mission might be.

Identity: Who Do We Think We Are?

We are what we value. What do worshipers most value about their congregations? What worshipers value is the best gauge of their identity. Because it is difficult to name just one favorite, we asked worshipers to choose up to three aspects of their congregation that they particularly value. Great diversity of opinion about the most treasured aspects of congregational life emerged. Almost half (47%) chose sharing the sacrament of Holy Communion (i.e., sharing in the Eucharist, the Lord's Supper). The second most-valued feature is the sermons, preaching, or homilies (38%). Finally, almost one-third (31%) value the traditional style of worship or music characteristic of their congregation. Other areas of congregational life were chosen by smaller numbers of people. About one in five worshipers chose each of the following aspects as their most valued: wider community care or social justice emphasis, contemporary style of music, and ministry for children and youth. (See Figure 9.1.)

Theologically conservative. As a whole, worshipers view themselves as theologically conservative. When asked about their stand on theological issues, half of all worshipers describe themselves as conservative (10% very conservative; 40% conservative). One-third say they are "right in the middle." Fewer worshipers assert that their views on theological issues are liberal (14%) or very liberal (4%).

A Vision for the Future

Possibilities for the future. Do worshipers believe their congregation has a clear vision, goals, or direction for its ministry and mission? More than three out of four (77%) say "yes" and most (66%) are committed to the congregation's direction. But one in five worshipers (24%) characterize their congregation as not having a vision or as having ideas but no clear goals or direction. (See Figure 9.2.)

Excitement about the future. Most of those attending worship (76%) are excited

WE ARE WHAT WE VALUE

Which of the following aspects of this congregation do you personally most value? (Mark up to *three* options.)

Sharing in Holy Communion, Eucharist, or the Lord's Supper	47%
Sermons, preaching, or homilies	38%
Traditional style of worship or music	31%
Wider community care or social justice emphasis	22%
Contemporary style of worship or music	20%
Ministry for children or youth	19%
Reaching those who do not attend church	15%
Bible study or prayer groups, other discussion groups	14%
Practical care for one another in times of need	13%
Openness to social diversity	13%
Social activities or meeting new people	12%
Prayer ministry for one another	8%
The congregation's school or preschool	6%
Adult church-school or Sabbath-school class	5%

Figure 9.1

about their congregation's future. Some are neutral (20%), but only a few are not excited (3%).[1]

Another indicator of hopefulness about the future. The largest percentage of worshipers (30%) assert that their congregation is moving in new directions. Another one in

1. This survey question did not appear on the Catholic version. Therefore, the responses do not include Catholic worshipers.

POSSIBILITIES FOR THE FUTURE

Does this congregation have a clear vision, goals, or direction for its ministry and mission?

I am not aware of such a vision, goals, or direction 14%

There are ideas but no clear vision, goals, or direction.. 10%

Yes, and I am strongly committed to them... 36%

Yes, and I am partly committed to them 30%

Yes, but I am not committed to them.. 11%

Figure 9.2

five (19%) picture their congregation as currently deciding on new directions. But one in ten (13%) report their congregation is faithfully maintaining past directions. A small minority (5%) feel the congregation needs to get back to the way things were done in the past. (See Figure 9.3.)

Is the congregation ready to try something new? The potential for change exists in most congregations: 62% of all worshipers believe their congregation is always ready to try something new. Yet three in ten (30%) are unsure if their congregation is ready to change, and 9% say their congregation is *not* ready for change.

Identity and Vision in Real-World Churches

How churches identify and label themselves reveals something about their values, commitments, and hopes for the future. Mission statements, taglines, and Web site banners reflect core aspects of a congregation's basic theology. Congregations with a strong identity tend to be healthy in many ways and carry that identity "in the rhythm and pace of the congregation's life together. The identity they share comes from God, who touches them as a people in a place."[2]

Examples of identity markers and mission statements from fifteen highly focused congregations show the diversity of how they are shaped as faith communities.[3] They identify themselves in these ways:

- "A community of Christ's followers changing the world"

- "A Christ-centered community, committed to reaching our city, country and world with the love of Jesus Christ"

- "Building in faith, as family, for the future"

- "People of God's Extravagant Welcome"

HOPEFULNESS ABOUT THE FUTURE

Of the following, which *one* best describes your opinion of the future directions of this congregation?

We need to get back to the way we did things in the past	5%
We are faithfully maintaining past directions	13%
We are currently deciding on new directions	19%
We are currently moving in new directions	30%
We need to rethink where we are heading	7%
Our future is very unclear or doubtful	2%
Don't know	23%

Figure 9.3

---

2. Carl S. Dudley, *Effective Small Churches in the Twenty-first Century* (Nashville: Abingdon Press, 2003), 132.

3. Analysis of responses across all congregations revealed that worshipers in the fifteen congregations listed in Figure 9.4 achieved the highest scores for survey items related to vision and identity. These worshipers were more likely to report that (a) their congregation has a clear vision for its ministry and mission, (b) they are strongly committed to that vision, and (c) they believe their congregation is currently moving in new directions.

They set forth a mission (or vision) to accomplish these things:

- "Help people believe in Jesus Christ, grow to their spiritual potential, and serve in ministry."

- "Cause God great joy by sharing his love with others as we have seen it in Jesus Christ."

- "Love God, Love People, Serve Both."

- "Be a real church of the real God to the real world."

FAST FACT

Worshipers who are strongly committed to their congregation's vision hold different values than worshipers with less commitment.

Vision-committed worshipers are more likely to value the sermons they hear (44% chose this as one of the three aspects of the congregation they value most; only 36% of less vision-committed worshipers did so). They also value the Bible study or prayer groups offered by their congregation more than others do (18% of the vision-committed worshipers vs. 11% of others).

These indicators of identity come from a diverse group of congregations—large and small, scattered across the country, and with varied denominational ties. This diversity demonstrates that worshipers in congregations of all denominations and faith groups can display a strong and widely shared view about who they are and what the future holds. (See Figure 9.4.)

What Matters?

A clear identity and captivating vision for the future propel congregations forward. Historically, mainline Protestant denominations have taken on a broad agenda, viewing themselves as transformers of culture. Conservative Protestant groups, on the other hand, have seen themselves as transforming individuals, with personal salvation as the vehicle for such change.[4] Most scholars agree that identity and

4. David Roozen and James Nieman, *Congregations, Identity, and Change* (Grand Rapids: Wm. B. Eerdmans Publishing Co., 2005), 588–624.

CONGREGATIONS WITH STRONG IDENTITY AND VISION

Conservative Protestant

First Church of the Nazarene, Chester, SC	http://www.nazarene.athissite.com/
North Webster Church of God, North Webster, IN	http://www.nwcog.com/
Needmore Bible Church, Needmore, PA	http://www.needmorebiblechurch.org/
Trinity Baptist Church, Abilene, TX	http://www.trinityabilene.com/
Church on the Hill, McMinnville, OR	http://www.hillchurch.com/

Mainline Protestant

Evangelical Reformed United Church of Christ, Frederick, MD	http://www.erucc.org/
Christ United Methodist Church, Selinsgrove, PA	http://www.christchurchselinsgrove.org/
Advent Presbyterian Church, Cordova, TN	http://www.adventpres.com/
Peace United Church of Christ, Duluth, MN	http://www.peaceucc.org/
Lower Valley Presbyterian Church, Califon, NJ	http://www.lowervalley.org/

Catholic

Sacred Heart Catholic Church, Omaha, NE	http://sacredheartomaha.org/
St. Mary Magdalene Catholic Church, Higley, AZ	http://www.smarymag.org/
St. Justin Martyr Catholic Church, Seminole, FL	http://www.st-justinthemartyr.org/
Our Lady of Mount Carmel Catholic Church, Herrin, IL	http://ourladyofmtcarmelherrin.com/
Church of Our Lady of Lourdes, Utica, NY	http://www.ourladyoflourdesutica.org/

Figure 9.4

vision continue to make a difference in the daily life of congregations. However broad or narrow the focus, congregations benefit from a deep understanding of who God is and what God is currently doing. Their ultimate task is articulating two things—what is our congregation's response to who God is, and what does God ask of us?

©hris Morgan www.cxmedia.com

CHAPTER 10

CONGREGATIONS AND WORSHIPERS
IN THE TWENTY-FIRST CENTURY

Why birds migrate and how they fly from point A to point B has stumped biologists for some time. But now scientists are exploring these questions by equipping birds with backpacks. This pioneering technology—a tiny bird-sized backpack with sensors weighing less than a dime—has yielded surprising findings. Some birds fly faster and farther than anyone thought possible. This new research helps scientists grasp how climate change may endanger various species of birds.[1]

For understanding worshipers, our point A was in April 2001, when we snapped the first picture of American worshipers. Just three months earlier George W. Bush had begun his first term as the forty-third president. The September 11 attacks were five months away and the Iraq War two years in the future. Microsoft had announced the release of Office XP, and somehow we lived without Facebook and Twitter.

Church attendance swelled in September 2001 as Americans sought to deal with the deaths of innocent people. Many observers felt these events would change the terrain of U.S. religious behavior and beliefs forever.

Now fast-forward to point B in 2008 and 2009, when we took another snapshot of

1. Cornelia Dean, "Charting Bird Migrations by Using Tiny Backpacks," *New York Times*, February 23, 2009.

worshipers and their congregations. This second portrait lets us see how societal shifts since 2001 affected religious organizations and participants. Some changes are subtle and some dramatic.[2] In this chapter, we present seven areas where we found notable change for worshipers and congregations since 2001. We also discuss five other areas of remarkable stability in congregational life.

Migrations between 2001 and Today

Increasing use of technology. One of the biggest changes since 2001 is that congregations have embraced the Internet as a way to enhance their mission. Only 43% of congregations had established a congregational Web site in 2001. That percentage almost doubled (77%) by 2008. (See Figure 10.1.)

Congregations use their Web sites as electronic billboards to help people in the community know about their services and programs. Their Web sites also help regular attendees know what is going on in the congregation. For example, 83% of congregations with Web sites post a calendar highlighting upcoming events. More than half list volunteer needs or service opportunities. Half post sermons—in text, audio, or video formats—and half (52%) post online newsletters. A small percentage (one in ten) allow worshipers to make financial contributions online. (See Figure 10.2.)

Many congregations (74%) also use e-mail to stay in touch with their members. Of those that do, most report they disseminate information (96%) and publicize events (84%) via e-mail. E-mail also enables congregations to inform their members about the joys and concerns of others in the congregation, help worshipers engage in ministries,

2. Researchers and others agree that congregational change at the national level is much slower than at the level of an individual congregation. The portrait of U.S. congregations changes incrementally. Most trends are long-term, lasting for ten to twenty years or more. We believe a snapshot of a national random sample of congregations should detect most significant shifts in religious life among worshipers and their congregations. Our assumption is based on congregational studies conducted by other U.S. sociologists (e.g., Mark Chaves, University of Arizona/Duke University) and by our research colleagues in Australia, who conducted the National Church Life Survey (NCLS). The NCLS comprises five national surveys of Australian worshipers since 1986. In their numerous publications (see www.ncls.org.au), NCLS researchers carefully document steady but modest change at the national level. The seven areas we highlighted as showing notable change were chosen based on statistical significance tests (in the case of the congregational profile data) and major differences in percentages between 2001 and 2008 (in the case of the worshiper data).

INCREASING USE OF TECHNOLOGY

	2008	2001
Established or maintained a Web site for the congregation	77%	43%
Use e-mail to communicate with attendees	74%	45%

Figure 10.1

THE CONGREGATION'S WEB SITE

Has a church calendar highlighting events	83%
Lists volunteer needs or service opportunities	54%
Has an online newsletter	52%
Offers sermon transcripts (audio, video, text)	48%
Offers an online giving option	9%

Note: Includes responses from the 77% of congregations with Web sites

Figure 10.2

offer opportunities to register for events, solicit feedback from worshipers, and send devotional messages. (See Figure 10.3.)

Diversifying worship. A majority of worshipers still choose traditional hymns as one of their three preferences for congregational worship, but the percentage of worshipers favoring traditional music has dropped from 61% in 2001 to 56% today. Among worshipers ages 25 to 44, just 45% prefer traditional hymns, so we expect this trend will continue.

Several changes suggest less formality in worship. Compared to 2001, fewer congregations today regularly include singing by a choir or soloist, Communion or the Lord's Supper, the use of hymnals or hymnbooks, and a written bulletin or service

HOW CONGREGATIONS USE E-MAIL

Disseminate information 96%

Publicize events.. 84%

Inform the congregation of joys and concerns.................................... 67%

Help members and guests engage in ministries................................. 67%

Offer opportunities to register for events.. 46%

Solicit feedback from worshipers 29%

Send devotional messages 20%

Note: Includes responses from the 74% of congregations that use e-mail to stay in touch with attendees.

Figure 10.3

MYTH TRAP

Worshipers are less engaged in their congregations now than in the past.

How worshipers participate in the congregation has changed very little since 2001. They are still involved in small groups, take on leadership responsibilities, and make regular financial contributions at about the same levels as before.

outline in their largest worship service. (See Figure 10.4.)

More care and advocacy by congregations. The involvement of congregations in activities and programs that serve members and people in the community has increased since 2001. The largest increase is in services for children and youth such as job training, literacy programs, scouting, and sports. In 2001, three in ten congregations provided such programs; today half do.

Art, music, and cultural activities increased at a similar pace. Three in ten congregations sponsored such activities in 2001. Today, almost half provide such culture-related activities. Four other areas increased almost as much: emergency

DIVERSIFYING WORSHIP

The largest (or only) worship service includes:	2008	2001
Singing by a choir or soloist	74%	87%
Hymnbooks	74%	85%
Communion, Eucharist, Lord's Supper	72%	85%
Written bulletin or service outline	60%	75%
Participation by teens	37%	55%

Figure 10.4

relief activities including food, meals, clothing, or other assistance for people in crisis, hobby and craft groups; other welfare and social service activities; and recreational and leisure activities. (See Figure 10.5.)

Worshipers themselves echo this change. In 2001, just 15% of worshipers cited the congregation's wider community care as one of the three factors they value; now, 22% affirm this value.

Decreasing financial strength despite stable size. Congregations are about the same size today as they were in 2001. More than two out of three congregations averaged 150 or fewer worshipers in 2001; the same number falls into that small-church category today. (See Figure 10.6.)

Evidence of declining congregational strength comes from a subjective view of the congregation's financial health.[3] In 2001, one-half of congregations were described as having a stable financial base, while one in three had an increasing financial base. Today, while the percentage deemed to be financially stable remains about the same, far fewer congregations (just 12%) are blessed with an increasing financial base. Almost one in three face a declining financial base. (See Figure 10.7.)

3. The congregational profile, which gathered facts and figures about the congregation and was completed by one person in each congregation, included a question about the financial viability of the congregation.

MORE CARE AND ADVOCACY BY CONGREGATIONS

	2008	2001
Emergency relief or material assistance (food, clothes for the needy)	87%	74%
Other social, recreational, or leisure activities	52%	42%
Other programs for children and youth (job training, literacy program, scouting, sports)	49%	31%
Art, music, or cultural activities or programs	44%	28%
Health-related programs and activities (blood drives, screenings, health education)	37%	29%
Other senior citizen programs or assistance (Meals on Wheels, transportation)	37%	29%
Other welfare, community service, or social action activities not mentioned here	30%	18%
Hobby or craft groups	29%	16%
Political or social justice activities (civil rights, human rights)	22%	14%
Substance abuse or 12-step recovery programs	20%	14%
Care for persons with disabilities (skills training, respite care, home care)	16%	10%
Animal welfare or environmental activities	11%	4%

Figure 10.5

We reviewed how congregations are financially supported in chapter 3. The total income congregations now receive is more than in 2001, even when adjusting for inflation. The median congregational budget almost doubled since 2001—from $121,000 to $226,000. Operating expenses climbed as well. More money flows into the typical congregation than before, but more money is expended. (See Figure 10.8.)

SIZE OF CONGREGATIONS REMAINS STABLE

Congregations with:	2008	2001
Fewer than 150 worshipers	69%	69%
150 to 300 worshipers	17%	19%
More than 300 worshipers	15%	12%

Figure 10.6

Older worshipers. In chapter 2, we noted that worshipers are older, on average, than the general population in the United States. But perhaps more important is the fact that the average worshiper today is older than the average worshiper in 2001. The average age of worshipers has increased from 50 in 2001 to 54 today. Two-thirds of worshipers are now 45 or older, up from six in ten in 2001. More worshipers today are retired (up from 25% in 2001 to 29% today), which reflects the aging of worshipers. (See Figure 10.9.)

More educated worshipers. Another demographic change is reflected in an increase in the percentage of worshipers who have graduated from college. Among those age 25 and up, this percentage increased from 38% in 2001 to 47% today.[4]

Less frequent attendance. Fewer worshipers today report attending worship services on a weekly basis. In 2001, 83% came to worship services "usually every week" or "more than once a week." That number has dropped to 76%. Most of that decline is among worshipers in Catholic parishes, where the percentage of weekly worshipers fell from 88% to 77%. Unlike in 2001, Catholic worshipers today do not attend more frequently than worshipers in Protestant churches. (See Figure 10.10.)

4. The change in the percentage of worshipers with a college degree (up 6 percentage points) was larger than the gain in the U.S. population during the same time frame (23% to 27%; up 4 percentage points).

WHICH STATEMENT BEST DESCRIBES YOUR CONGREGATION'S FINANCIAL SITUATION?

	2008	2001
We have an increasing financial base.	12%	29%
We have an essentially stable financial base.	57%	53%
We have a declining financial base.	29%	16%
Our financial situation is a serious threat to our ability to continue as a viable congregation.	1%	2%

Figure 10.7

HOW IS THE CONGREGATION FINANCIALLY SUPPORTED?

	2008	2001
Income from all sources	$210,450	$127,869
Income from individuals' donations	$167,105	$107,530
Total congregation budget	$225,880	$121,097
Congregation's operating expenses	$160,000	$102,074

Note: Median amount for most recent fiscal year before the survey. The 2001 figures are adjusted for inflation.

Figure 10.8

OLDER WORSHIPERS

	2008	2001	Change
Age 15–24	8%	10%	–2
Age 25–44	24%	30%	–6
Age 45–64	39%	36%	+3
Age 65 and older	30%	24%	+6
Median age	54	50	+4

Figure 10.9

Stability over Time

Megachurches. The popular media cover megachurches repeatedly and extensively, which might lead us to conclude that megachurches are pervasive and increasing in number. But that is not the case. In 2001, we found that just 4% of congregations fell into the megachurch category—having more than 1,000 in worship. Almost all of these were Catholic parishes, which are not typically included in the megachurch definition.[5] That picture remains the same today. In 2008, 2% of congregations reported worship attendance above 1,000, and again most of these were Catholic parishes.

Demographics. We have discussed the aging of U.S. worshipers and their increasing levels of education. Beyond that, there is considerable stability in the portrait of worshipers—their gender, marital status, and household composition remain unchanged.

Participating nonmembers. In 2001 we found that 11% of worshipers regularly

5. A megachurch is "a Protestant church that averages at least 2,000 total attendees in their weekend services" (Scott Thumma and Dave Travis, *Beyond Megachurch Myths* [San Francisco: Jossey-Bass, 2007], xviii). Some researchers use 1,000 attendees or more as the mark of a megachurch.

LESS FREQUENT WORSHIP ATTENDANCE

Weekly attendees:	2008	2001
All worshipers	76%	83%
Worshipers in Catholic parishes	77%	88%
Worshipers in other congregations	75%	78%

Figure 10.10

participated in their congregations but were neither members nor in the process of joining. While we expected that percentage to increase over time, the change was minimal. Today about 12% of worshipers are nonmembers. Yet differences based on the age of worshipers indicate that the percentage of participating nonmembers could grow in the future. Currently, one in ten worshipers age 45 or older are participating nonmembers, but twice as many younger worshipers (18%) are not members of their congregations.

Congregational involvement. Other than a decrease in weekly worship attendance, we found very little change in the extent and ways in which worshipers are involved in congregational activities. At both points in time, about four in ten worshipers hold leadership roles in their congregations; about four in ten worshipers participate in the congregation's small groups; and almost half give at least 5% of their income to the congregation. Worshipers' engagement in their congregations remains stable.

Congregational feedback. Worshipers are also very consistent in their comments about worship services, congregational activities, and their leaders. The percentages who experience God's presence, inspiration, and joy during worship services in their congregations continue unchanged, and large numbers at both times say their spiritual needs are being met in the congregation. Satisfaction with programs for children and youth remains unchanged. Large majorities in 2001 and now report their pastor, priest, or other leader is a good match for their congregation.

Who Speaks for Congregations?

In these pages, we describe the current state of American congregational life and resist the pull toward prescriptions for whatever ailments or struggles sacred communities face. Yet some worshipers and leaders may construct a story or narrative that interprets the trajectory we have just depicted. Is the story of congregational life one of decline that invites God's punishment? Or is it a prodigal-son narrative that says congregations will always remain part of God's larger purposes? In other words, how do we understand the changes described above? While either narrative can be argued to be true or authentic, our theological views, investments, and commitments color which perspective we tend to favor.

The ways we think about the past, present, and future of congregations are nested in an American way of viewing events. Andrew Murphy writes about how we use stories to interpret our country's past. He says they are "jeremiads"—stories of decline, like the prophecies of Jeremiah, the weeping prophet. He claims there are two types of American jeremiads: the traditionalist, which sees the past as completely virtuous and the present as problematic; and the progressive, which views the past as a source of our best ideals or principles, upon which we can rise to a better future. In the progressive jeremiad, the past is our nation's birthright, offering us hope and promise.[6]

6. Andrew R. Murphy, *Prodigal Nation: Moral Decline and Divine Punishment from New England to 9/11* (New York: Oxford University Press, 2009).

FAST FACT

**One in five Americans express no religious identity.[*]
Among those who do have a religious preference, a good number rarely—if ever—attend services.[†]**

The worshipers' views presented in this book reflect a world that is foreign to these unaffiliated and uninvolved people. Congregations in the twenty-first century face the challenge of reaching an increasing number of people who have little or no experience with religious institutions. How will your congregation respond?

[*] B. A. Kosmin and A. Keysar, American Religious Identification Survey 2008 (Hartford, CT: Trinity College), http://www.americanreligionsurvey-aris.org/reports/ARIS_Report_2008.pdf.
[†] C. Kirk Hadaway and Penny Long Marler, "How Many Americans Attend Worship Each Week? An Alternative Approach to Measurement," *Journal for the Scientific Study of Religion* 44, no. 3 (2005): 307–22.

Both American jeremiads acknowledge problems in the present. The traditionalist jeremiad asserts that we need to return to past ways of behaving and believing to address current difficulties. The progressive jeremiad, on the other hand, finds heroic examples of people facing predicaments and overcoming injustice in the imperfect past. These examples of triumph provide evidence that today's situation is not so dire that we cannot prevail. Both types of jeremiads reflect a tension between despair in the present and hope for future redemption.

Both jeremiad accounts express disappointment in the present. These accounts fail us if we have not lost something, but rather miss that something new is under way. Perhaps new forms of interaction, identity, and community—as powerful as anything in the past—are emerging. Thus, another account of our past, present, and future calls congregations to more faith-filled participation in what God is about in the world. Indeed, our research revealed areas where congregations are more successful in achieving their mission than in 2001, as well as areas where their strength has diminished.

Scientists studied monarch migration for more than thirty years before they discovered where the butterflies spent their winters. Eventually, Kenneth Brugger and his wife found a remote mountain in Mexico where the trees were so thick with butterflies they looked orange instead of green. But the man who discovered their secret location couldn't fully appreciate what he was seeing—he was colorblind.[7] Surely, as witnesses to the present picture of congregational life, we too can be colorblind to what we see.

Reality matters, and what people do with facts matters even more. This field guide asserts that congregations and their leaders can make data-driven decisions that make a difference. Worshipers across America have now told their story about what matters to them. They join the long tradition of people of faith who have always told stories that help them honor the past and give definition to the future. Some stories grow larger and more significant with time because they recount how we came to be the people of God.

7. "The Writer's Almanac," January 2, 2009, retrieved from newsletter@americanpublicmedia.org.

U.S. CONGREGATIONAL LIFE SURVEY METHODOLOGY

More than 500,000 worshipers in more than 5,000 congregations across America participated in the U.S. Congregational Life Survey, making it the largest survey of American worshipers ever conducted. Three types of surveys were completed in each participating congregation: (1) an attendee survey completed by all worshipers age 15 and older who attended worship services during the weekend the survey was given; (2) a congregational profile describing the congregation's facilities, staff, programs, and worship services completed by one person in the congregation; and (3) a leader survey completed by the pastor, priest, minister, rabbi, or other leader. Together the information collected provides a unique three-dimensional look at religious life in America.

The results presented in this book are from two national random samples of congregations. Each sample was identified by means of hypernetwork sampling. Using this method, individuals in a random sample of adults in the United States who reported that they attended worship at least once in the prior year were asked to name the place where they worshiped. Because the individuals comprised a random sample, the congregations they named comprise a random sample of congregations. Nominated congregations were verified and then invited to participate in the project. The first sample of congregations (Wave 1) was identified and recruited by the National Opinion Research Center at the University of Chicago and participated in the U.S. Congregational Life Survey in April 2001. The second sample (Wave 2) was identified and recruited by Harris Interactive and participated in the U.S. Congregational Life Survey in the fall of 2008 and the spring of 2009. This book focuses primarily on congregations and worshipers participating in Wave 2. Comparing results from Wave 2 to results from Wave 1 allowed us to examine change in congregational life at the national level.

Congregations in the national random sample that participated in 2001 were also invited (by Harris Interactive) to take part in Wave 2. Comparing results for congregations that participated in both Wave 1 and Wave 2 provided an opportunity to examine change at the congregational level.

Of 1,214 congregations nominated and verified in the first sample, 807 agreed to participate (66%), and 434 returned completed surveys from their worshipers in 2001 (54% of congregations that agreed to participate). (Congregations that chose not to participate gave a wide variety of reasons.) Worshipers in these congregations completed 122,043 attendee surveys. Of 1,330 congregations nominated and verified in the second sample, 201 agreed to participate (15%) and 148 returned completed worshiper surveys (74% of those that agreed). Worshipers in these congregations completed 36,468 surveys. Finally, 411 of the 434 congregations that participated in Wave 1 were verified and located in 2008. Of these, 145 agreed to participate in Wave 2 (35%), and 108 returned completed surveys from their worshipers (74% of those that agreed). These congregations returned 26,206 completed attendee surveys.

The size of these scientific statistical samples far exceeds the size of most national surveys. Studies designed to provide a representative profile of adults living in the United States typically include about 1,000 people.

In Wave 1 and Wave 2, denominations were also invited and encouraged to draw a random sample of their congregations. Denominational samples were large enough so that the results are representative of worshipers and congregations in each denomination. This allows denominations to compare their "typical" congregation and worshiper to congregations and worshipers in other denominations. Denominations participating in this oversampling procedure in Wave 1 were Church of the Nazarene, Evangelical

Lutheran Church in America, Presbyterian Church (U.S.A.), Roman Catholic Church, Seventh-day Adventist Church, Southern Baptist Convention, United Methodist Church, and United Church of Christ. In subsequent years, the Interdenominational Theological Center used the U.S. Congregational Life Survey with samples of predominantly black Protestant churches, Catholic parishes, and mosques, and the Episcopal Church conducted an oversample of Episcopal churches. Denominations sponsoring oversamples for Wave 2 were Church of God (Cleveland, Tennessee), Church of the Nazarene, Evangelical Lutheran Church in America, Presbyterian Church (U.S.A.), Seventh-day Adventist Church, United Methodist Church, and United Church of Christ.

Finally, many individual congregations and small groups of congregations have taken the survey. (See appendix 4 for details about taking the survey.) Results from these other congregations and samples are not included here.

Additional information about the methods used in this study is available on our Web site, www.USCongregations.org.

QUESTIONS AND ANSWERS

What level of analysis was used? Most of the information presented in this book is based on surveys completed by worshipers. That is, we examine the responses of individual worshipers. We discuss who worshipers are, what they are doing in their congregations, how they are involved in the community, and what they see for the future of the congregation.

We also include some information from two other surveys completed by one person in each congregation. First, information from the congregational profile describes the congregation's programs, services, facilities, staff, and finances. Second, the leader survey gathers information about the education and background of the key leader (pastor, priest, rabbi) in each congregation and his or her experiences in ministry. We weighted data from the congregational profile to account for size and nonresponse bias. Data from the leader survey were weighted to account for size. Because congregations were nominated for participation in this study by a random sample of adults, larger congregations (with so many more worshipers) were more likely to have been nominated. The weights we used counterbalanced this bias. Similarly, certain denominations and faith groups were underrepresented in the sample, and the weights also corrected for this bias.

How were the denominational families established? The three denominational families used in this book represent a common typology of congregations used by religion researchers. Congregations within each family are fairly similar to one another in terms of theology and belief, and they are less similar to congregations in other faith groups. Appendix 3 lists the denominations and faith groups participating in the U.S. Congregational Life Survey.

What is the difference between a mean and a median? A mean and a median are two ways to estimate the average of a set of numbers. Median refers to the middle number in an ordered series. For example, the median age for a group of people aged 12, 21, 28, 35, and 64 years would be 28 years—the middle score in the series. Mean refers to the mathematical average of values in a series; in the example, the mean age would be calculated by adding all the scores and dividing by the number of scores: (12 + 21 + 28 + 35 + 64) divided by 5, or 32 years.

How was congregational growth measured? Each participating congregation completed a congregational profile that asked for the average annual worship attendance for the last eight years (2001 to 2008). Because some congregations took the survey in 2008, worship attendance figures for that year were incomplete. Growth was measured as an average of two measures of the annual percentage of growth or decline in worship attendance: (1) between 2001 and 2008 (attendance in 2008 minus attendance in 2001, the difference divided by attendance in 2001) and (2) between 2001 and 2007. Thus, positive numbers indicate a congregation has more worshipers in 2008 than in 2001, and negative numbers indicate fewer worshipers. Some congregations did not report attendance figures for 2008 and/or for 2001. In such cases, growth was calculated based on the earliest and latest reported attendance figures.

My congregation would like to see how we compare with the U.S. results. Can we take the survey? Will the report help us identify our strengths? Yes! See appendix 4 for details about taking the survey.

How much difference is needed to indicate that my congregation is different from the national averages? In general, differences of 3% to 5% are considered statistically significant differences. That means that any difference less than that amount may be due entirely to random variation in the measures.

Can my congregation's results change? Yes. Although it is unlikely that your worshipers' responses will change rapidly, as your congregation changes—for example, adds new worshipers, programs, and staff; loses members (whether due to death, mobility, or other factors); discontinues ineffective or outdated programs; or experiences a changing financial situation—the views of your worshipers will change, too. Unless there has been considerable change in your congregation, we don't recommend reassessing your results (by retaking the survey) more often than every three to five years

DENOMINATIONS AND FAITH GROUPS OF PARTICIPATING CONGREGATIONS

Participating congregations come from these denominations and faith groups:

American Baptist Churches in the U.S.A.

Assemblies of God

Baptist (unspecified)

Baptist Bible Fellowship

Calvary Ministries International
   (Pentecostal)

Christian Church (Disciples of Christ)

Church of God (Anderson, Indiana)

Church of God (Cleveland, Tennessee)

Church of the Nazarene

Community of Christ (formerly
   Reorganized Church of Jesus Christ of
   Latter-day Saints)

Cooperative Baptist Fellowship

Cumberland Presbyterian Church

Duck River Association of Baptists

Episcopal Church

Evangelical Covenant Church

Evangelical Free Church of America

Evangelical Lutheran Church in America

Free Methodist Church of North America

Lutheran Church–Missouri Synod

Lutheran Congregations in Mission for
   Christ

Mennonite Church

Metropolitan Community Church

National Association of Congregational
   Christian Churches
National Baptist Convention, U.S.A., Inc.
Nondenominational congregations
Presbyterian Church (U.S.A.)
Reform Judaism
Reformed Church in America
Religious Society of Friends (Quaker)
Roman Catholic Church

Salvation and Deliverance International
Serbian Eastern Orthodox Church
Seventh-day Adventist Church
Southern Baptist Convention
Unitarian Universalist Association
United Church of Christ
United Methodist Church
Willow Creek Association

Ten Strengths of U.S. Congregations: Mapping Change

In *Beyond the Ordinary: Ten Strengths of U.S. Congregations* (Louisville, KY: Westminster John Knox Press, 2004), we detailed ten aspects of congregational vitality. There, we focused on strengths, believing that naming what makes congregations strong fosters greater effectiveness than identifying weaknesses. Changing the mind-set from "what's wrong with us" to "what's right with us" moves congregations toward achieving their mission. This shift celebrates the positives in congregational life and motivates worshipers and leaders to take necessary actions. Building on strength supplies the leverage for the next steps of a congregation's future.

Our research demonstrates that all congregations have strengths. Each of the ten strengths contributes to the health and vitality of individual congregations.

What are the ten factors that are important for successful congregations? Strong congregations (1) help their worshipers grow spiritually, (2) provide meaningful worship, (3) are places where worshipers participate in the congregation in many ways, (4) give worshipers a sense of belonging, (5) care for children and youth, (6) focus on the community, (7) help worshipers share their faith with others, (8) welcome new people, (9) rely on empowering congregational leadership, and (10) have a positive outlook on the future. These strengths are calculated from the responses of all worshipers in more than 5,000 congregations that participated in the U.S. Congregational Life Survey. (See Table 1.)

How were the ten strengths identified? In this book, we reported on congregations and their worshipers in four interrelated areas—spiritual connections, inside connections, outside connections, and identity connections. The ten strengths flow from those four areas and tap the essential strengths of congregations. This multifaceted approach allows congregations to find the areas in which they excel. Also, we are indebted to many congregational and denominational leaders, church consultants, and religious researchers who helped us inventory the characteristics of healthy and vital congregations.

How were the questions that make up each strength selected? We used a systematic method to determine the specific questions that make up each strength. First, we listed all survey questions that were designed to measure each strength. Second, we selected for inclusion in the measure the specific answers to each question that were most important. For example, when using the question about worshipers' private devotions, two answers were chosen because they are most reflective of growth in faith—spending time in private devotional activities either "every day or most days" or "a few times a week." Third, we subjected this pool of questions and specific answers for each strength to statistical analyses that allowed us to uncover those combinations that best measure that strength. We used Cronbach's coefficient alpha statistic (a measure of the reliability of a scale) to make this determination. Sometimes, questions that we thought would be significant in measuring a particular strength turned out to be relatively unimportant and were dropped. Cronbach's alpha for each strength is shown in Table 2. (A Cronbach's alpha could not be calculated on Welcoming New People because this index was based on a single survey item—the percentage of worshipers who began participating in the past five years.)

How are overall scores calculated? The overall score for each strength is calculated as the average (mean) of the questions that comprise that strength. The overall scores reported here are the averages of the means from all congregations that participated. We also calculated an overall score for each congregation using the answers of all worshipers who completed surveys there.

Can I compare the scores across strengths? No. Because the questions that comprise each index use widely different scales, they cannot be compared. That is, just because the average score on the Growing Spiritually Index is higher than the average score on the Meaningful Worship Index does *not* mean that congregations in general are doing better in the area of spirituality than in the area of worship. It *is* appropriate to compare the scores of different types of congregations on one index—for example, comparing large congregations to small ones on the Growing Spiritually Index.

Can I compare the Wave 1 (2001) and Wave 2 (2008 and 2009) scores? Yes! Table 2 shows the overall score for each strength as well as the scores on individual survey items comprising that strength. The overall picture is one of declining scores, with a few notable exceptions. Worshipers reported *more* involvement in their communities now than in 2001 (almost 8 percentage points higher in 2008 and 2009). While this is a reason to celebrate, three other areas were not as strong as before—Having a Sense of Belonging, Sharing Faith, and Welcoming New People. The smaller differences for the remaining six strengths place them in the "stable" category.

TEN STRENGTHS OF CONGREGATIONS

Growing Spiritually: Many worshipers are growing in their faith and feel the congregation meets their spiritual needs.

Meaningful Worship: Many worshipers experience God's presence, joy, inspiration, and awe in worship services and feel worship helps them with everyday life.

Participation in the Congregation: Many worshipers attend services weekly and are involved in the congregation.

Sense of Belonging: Many worshipers have a strong sense of belonging and say most of their closest friends attend the same congregation.

Caring for Children and Youth: Many worshipers are satisfied with the offerings for children and youth and have children living at home who also attend there.

Focusing on the Community: Many worshipers are involved in social service or advocacy activities and work to make their community a better place to live.

Sharing Faith: Many worshipers are involved in evangelism activities and invite friends or relatives to worship.

Welcoming New People: Many worshipers began attending in the past five years.

Empowering Leadership: Many worshipers feel the congregation's leaders inspire others to action and take into account worshipers' ideas.

Looking to the Future: Many worshipers feel committed to the congregation's vision and are excited about the congregation's future.

Table 1

COMPARING STRENGTH MEASURES: 2001 VS. 2008

Strength	2001	2008	Change
Growing Spiritually (coefficient alpha = .77)	47%	44%	–3
Much growth in faith through participation in activities of the congregation	43%	35%	–8
Spend time at least a few times a week in private devotions	72%	69%	–3
Feel their spiritual needs are being met in the congregation	84%	84%	0
Report Bible study and prayer groups are one of the three most valued aspects of the congregation	21%	17%	–4
Report prayer ministry of the congregation is one of the three most valued aspects of the congregation	16%	14%	–2
Meaningful Worship (coefficient alpha = .86)	62%	60%	–2
Always or usually experience God's presence during services	78%	78%	0
Always or usually experience inspiration during services	78%	76%	–2
Rarely experience boredom during services	69%	65%	–4
Always or usually experience awe during services	25%	24%	–1
Always or usually experience joy during services	79%	75%	–4

Table 2

COMPARING STRENGTH MEASURES: 2001 VS. 2008 (cont.)

Strength	2001	2008	Change
Rarely experience frustration during services	73%	66%	−7
Report worship helps them with everyday life	56%	61%	+5
Report sermons or homilies are one of the three most valued aspects of the congregation	39%	37%	−2
Participating in the Congregation (coefficient alpha = .82)	**60%**	**58%**	**−2**
Attend worship services usually every week or more often	81%	79%	−2
Involved in one or more small groups (e.g., Sunday school, prayer or Bible study, discussion groups, fellowships)	67%	67%	0
Hold one or more leadership roles in the congregation (e.g., board member, teacher, leading worship)	57%	60%	+3
Often participate in decision making in the congregation	33%	26%	−7
Give 5% or more of net income to the congregation	63%	57%	−6
Sense of Belonging (coefficient alpha = .74)	**37%**	**30%**	**−7**
Have a strong sense of belonging to the congregation that is growing	58%	49%	−9
Most of closest friends attend the same congregation	19%	14%	−5

Table 2

COMPARING STRENGTH MEASURES: 2001 VS. 2008 (cont.)

Strength	2001	2008	Change
Participated in congregational activities more than two years ago	33%	27%	–6
Caring for Children and Youth (coefficient alpha = .65)	**50%**	**53%**	**+3**
Satisfied with offerings for children and youth	58%	55%	–3
Report ministry for children or youth is one of the three most valued aspects of the congregation	16%	18%	+2
Percentage of children and youth living at home who worship in the same congregation	77%	85%	+8*
Focusing on the Community (coefficient alpha = .81)	**33%**	**41%**	**+8**
Involved in social service or advocacy groups through the congregation	26%	32%	+6
Involved in social service or advocacy groups outside the congregation	28%	42%	+14
Contributed money to a charitable group other than the congregation	66%	74%	+8
Report the congregation's wider community care and advocacy are one of the three most valued aspects of the congregation	11%	19%	+8

Table 2

COMPARING STRENGTH MEASURES: 2001 VS. 2008 (cont.)

Strength	2001	2008	Change
Report the congregation's openness to social diversity is one of the three most valued aspects of the congregation	8%	13%	+5
Worked with others to try to solve a community problem in last year	21%	24%	+3
Voted in the presidential election	71%	84%	+13**
Sharing Faith (coefficient alpha = .90)	**32%**	**28%**	**−4**
Involved in evangelism activities of the congregation	23%	24%	+1
Feel at ease talking about their faith and seek opportunities to do so	24%	20%	−4
Invited friend or relative to worship in past year	60%	50%	−10
Report ministry to the unchurched is one of the three most valued aspects of the congregation	22%	18%	−4
Welcoming New People	**33%**	**27%**	**−6**
Percentage of worshipers who began attending in the last five years			
Empowering Leadership (coefficient alpha = .84)	**49%**	**43%**	**−6**
Feel the congregation's leaders encourage them to use their gifts	41%	33%	−8
Feel the leader takes into account the ideas of others	54%	47%	−7

Table 2

COMPARING STRENGTH MEASURES: 2001 VS. 2008 (cont.)

Strength	2001	2008	Change
Describe the leadership style of the pastor or priest as one that inspires others	50%	47%	−3
Believe there is a good match between the pastor or priest and the congregation	53%	46%	−7
Looking to the Future (coefficient alpha = .82)	**41%**	**37%**	**−4**
Feel congregation has a clear vision and goals and is strongly committed to them	42%	40%	−2
Have a sense of excitement about the congregation's future	33%	26%	−7
Believe the congregation is already moving in new directions	32%	30%	−2
Believe the congregation is always ready to try new things	56%	52%	−4

* "Percentage of children and youth living at home who worship in the same congregation" was calculated somewhat differently in 2008, and these changes may account for the difference seen.

** "Voted in the presidential election" was assessed in 2001 asking about the 2000 election. In 2008, some worshipers took the survey before the 2008 election and told us about plans to vote. Others took the survey after the election and told us whether they had voted. These differences may account for the difference seen.

Table 2

The U.S. Congregational Life Survey: A Tool for Discovering Your Congregation's Strengths

Why conduct a survey of your congregation?
- To find out who your worshipers are and what they value

- To consider new missions or programs

- To renew or re-evaluate your strategic plan

- To deal with change when your congregation is growing or declining

- To get ready to call a new pastor

- To help a new pastor learn more about the congregation

Who will see our answers? They are completely confidential; unless you choose to share your results with others, no one outside your congregation will see them. You will send your surveys directly back to our research office. We will use an identification number to help us keep track of your congregation's responses, but individual answers are all confidential—in fact, we ask worshipers not to put their names on the survey. We will combine the responses of all of your worshipers and provide summary reports telling you what they said.

How should we give the survey? We can't afford to mail it to every member. The survey is designed to be given in worship on a typical Sunday or other day of worship. Giving the survey in worship is an efficient way to take a snapshot of your congregation, including regular worshipers, those who come less often, and visitors. If your congregation has more than one weekly service, the survey should be given in each.

Who should participate? Every worshiper who is at least fifteen years old should take part in the survey, including ushers, members of the choir, and others who help lead the service.

How much time will this require? Most worshipers can complete the survey in fifteen minutes. Each question is in a quick-response format so that worshipers do not have to write out their answers. We suggest setting aside about twenty minutes to allow time for explaining, distributing, and collecting the surveys.

How can we fit it in our worship service? Congregations have found a variety of ways to give the survey in worship. Many have found that it works well to set aside the last twenty minutes of each scheduled worship service to distribute the survey. Then worshipers can leave when they have finished. Our experience shows that if you let worshipers take the surveys home with them, few will return them. To make sure your portrait is accurate, it's essential to give the survey during worship.

When should we conduct the survey? It's your decision when to conduct the survey. Select the week that is most convenient for your congregation. It's best to pick a week that is typical. Giving the survey on Mother's Day or on a holiday weekend, for example, won't give you an accurate portrait if more visitors than normal attend or if many of your frequent attendees are away.

What will we get when we participate?

- Two customized, color reports with detailed profiles of your worshipers (their involvement in the congregation and community, their values, and their hopes for the future) and of your congregation (its unique strengths, especially compared to others of similar size and faith group).

- Two videos providing step-by-step instructions for interpreting the reports. They are designed to facilitate group discussion and help leaders identify congregational strengths.

- Two leader's guides with helpful ideas and tools for making the most of your congregation's reports.

- Two books summarizing the key national findings: *A Field Guide to U.S. Congregations: Who Is Going Where and Why* and *Beyond the Ordinary: 10 Strengths of U.S. Congregations* (both published by Westminster John Knox Press).

What will this cost? The current fees are listed on our Web site at www.USCongregations.org. You also may call 1-888-728-7228, ext. 2040, to learn more. We will send you all the surveys you need (forms are available in English, Spanish, and Korean), pens to complete them, and instructions for giving the survey in worship. You will need to pay for shipping to return the completed surveys to us for processing.

What about other questions we have? How can we sign up? To obtain general information, visit www.USCongregations.org, or if you're ready to get started, call 1-888-728-7228, ext. 2040.

What is U.S. Congregations? U.S. Congregations is a religious research group housed in the offices of the Presbyterian Church (U.S.A.) in Louisville, Kentucky, staffed by religious researchers and sociologists who are conducting the U.S. Congregational Life Survey.

THE INTERNATIONAL CONGREGATIONAL LIFE SURVEY AND THE U.S. CONGREGATIONAL LIFE SURVEY

The International Congregational Life Survey (ICLS) was initiated in 1999 as a collaborative effort of four countries. Extending the National Church Life Survey (NCLS) used earlier in Australia, the aim was to provide mission resources for congregations and parishes based on results from a survey of church attendees in four nations. The ICLS project was conducted in April and May 2001, with more than 12,000 congregations and 1.2 million worshipers participating. Each congregation invited all worshipers to complete a survey. The congregations also completed a congregational profile form, and the key leader in each congregation answered questions as well. Survey results were used to provide individualized reports to each participating congregation and to produce books, research reports, and other resources about religious life in the twenty-first century.

The 2001 ICLS was conducted by the following agencies and people:

Australia: National Church Life Survey (NCLS; http://www.ncls.org.au/) sponsored by ANGLICARE NSW of the Anglican Church in Australia, the New South Wales

Board of Mission of the Uniting Church in Australia, and the Australian Catholic Bishops Conference: Dean Drayton (convener of the ICLS steering committee), John Bellamy, Keith Castle, Howard Dillon, Robert Dixon, Peter Kaldor (founding director of NCLS), Ruth Powell, Tina Rendell, and Sam Sterland

England: Churches Information for Mission (CIM): Phillip Escott, Alison Gelder, and Roger Whitehead

New Zealand: Church Life Survey–New Zealand (CLS-NZ) is a subcommittee of the Christian Research Association of New Zealand: Norman Brookes

United States: U.S. Congregational Life Survey conducted by U.S. Congregations and supported by Lilly Endowment Inc., the Louisville Institute, and the Research Services office of the Presbyterian Church (U.S.A.): Deborah Bruce, Cynthia Woolever, Keith Wulff, Ida Smith-Williams

The second wave of the U.S. Congregational Life Survey (fall of 2008 and spring of 2009) was conducted by U.S. Congregations, supported by the Lilly Endowment, the Louisville Institute, and the Research Services office of the Presbyterian Church (U.S.A.): Deborah Bruce, Cynthia Woolever, Ida Smith-Williams, Joelle Anderson, Hilary Harris, and other staff